# BEEN THERE, Should've DONE THAT

## 995 Tips for Making the Most of College

4th Edition

Suzette Tyler

Front Porch Press
Bath, Michigan

# BEEN THERE, *Should've* ∧ DONE THAT

Copyright 1997, 2001, 2008, 2017 by Front Porch Press
Written by Suzette Tyler
Cover by Another Design Company
Design by Haas-Wittmann Design

Excerpt from Levitz/Noel National Dropout Study, 1991, by permission of USA Group, Noel/Levitz, Iowa City, Iowa. Some quotes have been edited for clarity and brevity.
Any references to registered trademarks incorporated herein are purely coincidental. These references are not made for the purpose of drawing upon the goodwill and intrinsic value of such trademarks.

Published by Front Porch Press, 1724 Vassar Drive Lansing, Michigan 48912
Phone: 517-487-9295  Fax: 517-487-0888  Email: styler@voyager.net  Website: www.frontporchpress.com

ISBN 978-0-9656086-9-5
Library of Congress Catalog Card Number: 96-62016
Printed in USA

# Acknowledgements

- The University Undergraduate Division of Michigan State University whose staff is dedicated to helping freshmen and sophomore students find their path to success and where my inspiration for this book began.

- The countless students and grads who have generously shared their time, insight and experiences over the years, to make this book what it is.

- Frances Kaneene—truly an adviser's adviser, whose experience and thoughtful reflection I always value.

- Liz Spaedt, who has always been willing to lend a hand or an ear, while keeping my feet on the ground—mostly.

- Kelly McCarthy, whose talent and patience made this update happen.

- Steven Harrelson, who reminded me how much college students need this information.

- My family, Adam, Tara, Josh, Sandra, and particularly Gary—for their love and support.

- Ely, Max and Gus—my motivation for "keepin' it going" for the next generation of college students.

# COTENTS

# Introduction

As they say, the more things change, the more they stay the same. In what seems like a 'nanosecond', technology has become interwoven into the everyday academic and social interactions of students and faculty across America. With that, the strategies and opportunities for success have expanded, as have the distractions and amount of information to sift through. In this fourth edition, students continue to offer their 'should'ves' and could'ves' and their advice continues to be as 'expert' as it gets. With a little editing here and there, their revelations and confessions are refreshingly insightful and often more encompassing than might be found in an adviser's office. The following pages will help campus newcomers discover, sooner rather than later, how to make the most of their college years. My thanks to all who shared their wisdom.

-S. Tyler

**"The problem with college is that you figure it out about the time you're ready to graduate."**

Senior, Economics, University of Florida

" I was pretty busy concentrating on my social life during orientation and welcome week. Attending information sessions definitely wasn't a priority. Unfortunately, I missed a few 'key points' that might have made life a little easier ... like the admissions requirements to the college of business! "

Junior, Communications, Michigan State University

# The 'Orientation' Express

## To Do's . . . and To Don'ts

**Pick an early session.** I waited until late in the summer so I could go to orientation with a friend. Forget that! All the courses were closed.

Sophomore, Advertising, University of Florida

**I 'friended' a couple people on Facebook** who I'd hit it off with at orientation. We kept in touch over the summer and bounced a lot of questions off one another. It was a relief to know I'd have some 'friends' on campus when I got there.

Sophomore, Environmental Science, Temple University

**Don't blow off all the welcome week stuff!** Sign up for activities and clubs that look even remotely interesting. You'll get all their emails and can decide later which to join. Just make sure to join something…it makes college more fun.

Junior, Marketing, Northern Illinois University

**Everyone was scrambling to figure out what courses to enroll in** while they were standing in line waiting for an adviser. For me, it was a breeze. I'd spent a lot of time on the website checking out majors and course descriptions before I came so I had a list of exactly what courses I was interested in.

Sophomore, Construction Management, Michigan State University

**Use a map to schedule classes.** I didn't . . . and spent a semester running from one end of campus to the other.

Sophomore, Psychology, UCLA

At orientation **I found out who I needed to talk to** about writing for the school newspaper and contacted them. By the time recruiting meetings were held several weeks into the fall semester, I had already written an article under my own by-line and was an 'old-timer' on the staff.

Junior, Journalism, University of Michigan

# A guaranteed JUMP-START

**I felt totally out of sync . . .** I didn't know anyone, didn't have a major, didn't know anything about anything....and I'd probably *still* be trying to figure out how to use the college websites! My University 101 class saved me! I made friends, discovered majors, met professors, and found campus resources that I probably never would have known existed.

Junior, Early Childhood Education, Miami University, Ohio

**Until I got involved in an incredible program** with cool activities and great academic support, I was lost. If I'd actually read my emails or checked out the website before school started, I could have been part of the program from day one.

Sophomore, Lansing Community College

Freshman program names differ on each campus—i.e., Freshman Seminar, Learning Communities, FIG—Freshman Interest Group, Mentoring Programs, TRIO, etc. Ask an adviser. (There is often limited space available.)

*"I NEVER read my email in high school. In college, email is HUGE…you HAVE to read it!*

Colleges put extra dollars, faculty, and advisers into programs to help freshmen succeed…**but you have to know about them!** *READ* every email and any other communication you get. Plus, explore both the college's website and your major's website.

The Adviser

**Don't 'skip' *anything* at orientation,** especially sessions that explain how to use the websites and apps you'll need! It can be really confusing if you have to learn it on your own.

Sophomore, Undecided, Michigan State University

**Ya gotta *BE THERE*. . .** not on your phone texting friends and family back home! Talk to the people around you. Ask questions. A lot of good information came just from talking to other students.

Sophomore, Sports Marketing, Xavier University

**Get rid of a course you're dreading** by taking it at a community college during the summer before classes start. I wish I had . . . my math course sucked up so much time during the first semester that I got crappy grades in everything.

Junior, Psychology, Southern Illinois University

**Keep your eyes open for ATMs** while you're on campus so you can figure out what debit card you want and where to do your banking.

Sophomore, Computer Science, University of Michigan

*"Taking placement tests online before orientation makes an already nerve-wracking experience less stressful."*

## Placement Tests . . . DON'T GUESS!!!

I must have been psychic when I took the placement tests. I guessed at everything and ended up in classes that were over my head . . . BIG MISTAKE!!

Junior, Environmental Science, Indiana University

Note: If there's a chance you can "place out" of a requirement and placement results are "suggested" rather than mandatory—guess away.

"I was like 'this room is a single ... right?' WROOONG!"

Sophomore, Engineering, Notre Dame

# Dorm Details

DORM DETAILS

*"Ya gotta decorate! You spend a lot of time there . . ."*

## PINTEREST RULES!

**My plan for decorating our room was awesome!** My roommate's plan was based on FAFSA loans and a comforter from home. I quickly dumped the designer stuff. Our room's fine and we get along great.

Sophomore, Nursing, University of Michigan

**My friend's room had a bar** that he built around a $2000 fish tank, and the biggest TV I've ever seen . . . cool, but ridiculous.

Graduate, Professional Writing, Michigan State University

**All you need are cheap posters,** Christmas lights and a fan . . .

Sophomore, Hospitality, Georgia State University

## Moving In Musts

**"Pay the extra fee to move in a day early.** When the cars are lined up and the elevator's jammed, you'll be glad you did."

**"If you're the first to move in,** don't grab the best bed, desk, dresser and closet. It won't impress your new roommate."

**"Report *any* room damage** *before* you move in so that you won't be charged for it at the end of the year."

**"Don't try to save bucks** buying a used rug unless it's *really* clean. Old rugs are killers if you have allergies."

**"Don't pound nails in anything** without permission."

## Housing - Options & Opinions

**'Quiet Floors'** are the way to go. You can always study in your own room and screw around on another floor.

DePaul University

**Community bathrooms** are great. There's no waiting when you need to use it, no conflict over whose turn it is to clean it and it's a great place to hear what's happening.

University of Illinois

**Freshman dorms** are awesome! Doors are always open ... people are friendly.

Ball State University

**Substance-free dorms** are just a lot of people having fun without all the garbage that comes with drinking.

Wake Forest University

**Single rooms** are okay for sophomores, but not freshmen. It's harder to meet people and there's no one to go to dinner with.

University of Michigan

**All-girl dorms** aren't much different than living in a sorority house.

John Carroll University

**Co-ed by floor or room,** but I'd definitely say single-sex by bathroom!

University of Michigan

# MAKING BIG Small

I'm in a 'living/learning' dorm—everyone lives in the same dorm and most of our classes are together. I was worried that it might get old real fast, but it's been great. My friends who aren't in this program spend day after day in huge lectures and never see anyone they know. I know everyone, including the faculty. **It's like a small college with Big Ten sports.**

Sophomore, Lyman Briggs College, Michigan State University

*"You might not like dorm food, but it's already paid for."*

## Food for Thought

**There are great restaurants** in this town and they all deliver to the dorms. I couldn't figure out where all my money had gone my first year until I realized I'd eaten it!

Sophomore, Nursing, University of Michigan

**Buffets are killers** if you have no willpower. There *IS* healthy food in the dining hall, you just have to choose it.

Junior, Accounting, Grand Valley State University

**Don't sign up for more than two meals a day** unless you plan on never eating out and making every breakfast . . . *riiiight!*

Senior, English, Rutgers

*"If your mom refrains from cooking for about two years before you go to college, you'll love dorm food."*

# ZAP-A-MEAL . . . when the menu sucks.

**Bar Pizza**
Pita bread or bagel (deli bar)
Marinara sauce (pasta bar)
Cheese (salad bar)
Veggies (salad bar)
*Zap in microwave.*

**Grilled Cheese Sandwich**
Toast two slices of bread
Snag some cheese (slices from
deli bar or grated from the
salad bar) *Zap in microwave.*

**Steamed Veggies au Gratin**
Veggies (salad bar) *Place in a
bowl with water. Cover with
second bowl and ZAP.* Cheese
(salad bar) *Place in a bowl
with water to thin and ZAP.
Pour over veggies.*

**Baked Apples**
Slice apples *Place in a bowl.*
Add cinnamon, sugar
(optional: butter and raisins).
*Cover with a second bowl.
Zap in microwave.*

*Shhh . . . bring a Ziploc bag and grab veggies and cheese for your bookbag.*

*"The 'Freshman 15' isn't from dorm food. It's alcohol
and ordering pizza when you're trashed at 3:00 A.M."*

## Healthy U

**You're at the mercy of vending machines** and Red Vines if you don't keep your room stocked with lots of healthy snacks.  Mindless munching runs rampant when you're stressed and have a paper due…or you're just plain bored.

Sophomore, Political Science, Lehigh University

**There are tons of easy recipes online** for making meals in your dorm room… from gluten/dairy-free chocolate cake in a coffee mug to veggie pizza bagels.

Junior, Accounting, Grand Valley State University

**I gotta get sleep** or I'm pretty much non-functioning. I make myself study during the day so I can keep 'late-nighters' down to a minimum.

Freshman, Criminal Justice, University of Memphis

**Anywhere else you'd be paying** for a health club . . . the workout facility here is top notch and you can work your butt off for free.

Sophomore, Biology, Grand Valley State University

**From little leagues, to middle school, to high school,** I always played competitive sports. My biggest mistake was not taking time for it in college.

Graduate, Sociology, Purdue University

**I like exercise when it's called something else**—tennis, ice skating, swing dance. The only way I'm consistent is if I enroll in a class where attendance is taken.

Sophomore, Psychology, University of Michigan

**All you do in college is sit!** I try to walk or ride my bike wherever I go.

Sophomore, Psychology, University of Michigan

# ON/OFF CAMPUS?

I couldn't wait to live in an apartment, but looking back, it was really more fun in the dorm. I met tons of people and there were more things to do . . . plus, the bathrooms were cleaner.

Graduate, Marketing, University of Wisconsin

**Don't move off campus** until you have a base of friends. It's isolating and you never hear about anything, whether it's good parties or good classes.

Sophomore, Construction Management, Michigan State University

**How 'worth it' is the *college experience?*** It's a hekuva lot cheaper to live off campus and a lot easier to study and sleep.

Sophomore, Psychology, UCLA

Once I moved out of the dorm, I was done. It's so easy not to go to class. **I never ate!** At least the dorm had meals. Plus, you need a car. That means gas and insurance and whatever . . .

Ex-Sophomore, Engineering, Central Michigan University

> Face it!
> To live with anyone 24 hours a day
> in a room the size of a closet
> is gonna bring on some tense moments,
> friend or not.

Junior, Sociology, University of Colorado

# Roommate Roulette

## Going in 'Blind'

**I'm from Des Moines and pretty conservative . . .** I took one look at this kid's posters and the clothes in his closet and thought 'NO WAY.' That was four years ago and we're still roommates. It's been cool . . . and I've grown.

Senior, Business, University of Iowa

**Every part of his body was pierced**—*EVERY* part—and he loved to show *everyone*. Between that, the punk music he went nuts to and the porno pics he also loved to show, it was a little tense. But looking back, it was only a few months out of my life and I have stories I can tell forever.

Sophomore, Undecided, Princeton University

**The wild and crazy person in Facebook** was not who showed up in my dorm room—thank God! Well, she's a little crazy . . . but that works.

Sophomore, Nutritional Sciences, Penn State University

**I had more problems** with the roommate from home than the one who was a complete stranger.

Senior, Packaging, Michigan State University

**Nothing ventured, nothing gained.** If it works out, you've made a friend for life. If it doesn't, it's only temporary.

Junior, Sociology, University of Colorado

**My roommate was an only child** and I was raised with three brothers. We drove each other nuts . . . but I actually missed her over the summer.

Senior, English, DePaul University

*"People aren't as considerate with friends as they are with strangers."*

Sophomore, Biophysics, University of Pennsylvania

## A 'Sure Thing'?

**I loved rooming with my best friend;** together we were ready to conquer anything. There was never that awkward period of getting to know each other or not feeling completely comfortable in your own room. It was nice to know what to expect—I never had to worry about whether she was with a guy or throwing a party or whatever . . .

Graduate, Professional Writing, Michigan State University

**My best friend met a guy** the first week of school and was gone most of the time. I might just as well have roomed alone!

Junior, Information Technology, University of Virginia

I roomed with a high school friend and we ended up barely speaking. I still had to go home to the same town where we both had the same friends . . . her mom knew my mom, her dad was my dad's client . . . **blah, blah, blah.** It wasn't worth it.

Junior, Business, Miami University

*"Don't expect too much . . . your roommate won't neccessarily be your best friend. That's okay."*

## Whatever Works

**My best friend and I requested the same dorm,** but not the same room. It was great because we ended up having friends individually and together. If I needed a familiar face or wanted to get out of the room, there was always someplace to go.

Junior, Psychology, Southern Illinois University

**I'm a wimp . . .** I wouldn't have had the courage to go to an out-of-state college if my friend wasn't going too. We were roommates but we shared a suite with two other girls so it was kind of like having the best of both worlds.

Junior, English, Indiana University

College is a good time to become the person you want to be. People accept you for who you are now, not who you were **in the third grade.**

Graduate, Marketing, University of Wisconsin

" It bugs the hell out of you
when your roommate's boyfriend
is in the room ALL the time,
even if he's a nice guy. "

Senior, English, Aquinas College

# Before It Gets *Ugly*

## The 'R' Word . . .

**You don't have to hang out with him,** you don't have to like him, but you do have to RESPECT him.

Junior, History, Notre Dame

**I had an incredible roommate all four years.** She was so easy to live with because before doing anything she always asked a question, 'Do you mind if . . . ?'

Graduate, Engineering, Iowa State University

## Cutting Through THE BULL . . .

The biggest mistake that roommates make
is that instead of just telling the other person what
they're mad about, they do something to get even . . .
so then everybody's mad and it just snowballs.

Junior (R.A.), Engineering, University of Miami

## Compromise . . .

**Take a break.** My roommate studied constantly—*in the room!* It was like a monastery. We're all in college to study, but there are times you need to do it elsewhere.

Sophomore, Education, Vanderbilt University

**My roommate had this 'need'** to make our room 'Party Central' all hours of the day and night. I was too gutless to suggest anything as nerdy as 'quiet hours.' It lasted until grades came . . . At least this nerd's still in school.

Junior, Geology, Arizona State University

**The kid was *glued* to the Internet** . . . that monitor light was never off. About three in the morning, I'd want to kill him!

Junior, Biology, University of Michigan

## Borrowing Boundaries . . .

**Set limits.** After letting my roommate borrow a sweater, my closet became a 'free-for-all,' especially if I left for the weekend. Make it clear that it's an 'ask first' policy and set a specific time that you 'need' it returned.

Senior, Psychology, Adelphi University

**Clean it.** Sharing clothes starts out as a great deal—until the sweater you were planning to wear smells like a gym bag or a brewery.

Senior, Business, Northern Illinois University

## Know When to Throw in the Towel . . .

**Don't drag it out.** My first clue should have been the day I arrived and found the entire room rearranged and my desk in the hall! It was downhill from there. If it's bad to start with, it'll only get worse. There are usually a few 'no show' spaces available in the fall. Request one.

Junior, Psychology, Southern Illinois University

**Gut it out.** It's just where you sleep. Spend time in other rooms or chalk the semester up as 'an experience.' It'll give you time to find a roommate you do like for the next semester.

Senior, Human Development, University of Connecticut

## TOP 10 Ways To Make Your Roommate Happy

**10**   Buy your own shampoo and deodorant—and use it.

  **9**   Wash your cereal bowl and socks before they're green and fuzzy.

  **8**   Keep your wet towel off the beds.

  **7**   Keep visits from high school friends down to something less than a week.

  **6**   Don't hit the "snooze" a thousand times for an eight o'clock you're not going to anyway.

  **5**   Don't. Eat. Your roommate's food.

  **4**   When your roomie's sleeping, turn your cell phone on vibrate and turn off the volume on your computer.

  **3**   Remember, it's a *dorm room*, not a romantic hideaway.

  **2**   Don't disappear when it's time to pay for the pizza . . . or anything else.

  **1**   **Flush.**

" I went to preschool
with the same kids
I graduated with from high school.
I never had a moment of trying
to figure out where I fit in—
until college! "

Sophomore, Economics, Williams College

# Bummers

**I cried everyday for the first month.** I couldn't even call home because I couldn't talk without sobbing. You just want to sit and do nothing . . . and that's the worst thing you can do. Force yourself to get busy.

Junior, Psychology, Southern Illinois University

**The hardest thing to get used to** is doing things alone. In high school I never even went to the bathroom alone much less *ate* alone. You have to learn to walk up to people and start talking.

Junior, Chemical Engineering, M.I.T.

**Don't go home the first month.** It only makes it harder when you come back. Besides, there's a lot going on and everyone is anxious to make friends.

Junior, Engineering, Notre Dame

**You have to put yourself out there.** Dorm 'icebreakers' and floor activities can be a little nerdy but they're good for meeting people.

Junior, Psychology, Georgetown University

**It's a bonding thing . . . friendships are made when you're hanging around doing nothing.**

Junior, Social Work, Rutgers University

*"I was trying so hard to make friends that I wasn't me."*

**Long distance relationships are tough to pull off.** The biggest mistake I made was having a girlfriend at another school the first two years. Neither of us really enjoyed college. It makes you older than you are.

Senior, English, Denison University

**There's no privacy in the dorms.** The first year was like not being able to breathe. I eventually found a family off campus who needed a babysitter and it was like reconnecting with the real world . . . kids, pets, houses. They've become my family away from home. It's really a nice break from the dorm.

Sophomore, Physical Therapy, Northwestern College

# Lost in Cyber Space

My high school friends went to other colleges and I really missed them. I spent all of my free time Facebooking and texting each of them daily. It began to seem like **they were having a lot more fun than I was. . .** which they were, because they were doing more than just sitting around their rooms on Facebook and texting me!

Sophomore, Nutritional Science, Penn State University

## "It ain't easy being green . . . " —Kermit the Frog

**Here I was 1,000 miles from home** dealing with people who had funny accents, piercings and sexual preferences I hadn't encountered before. Late-night talks in the girls bathroom opened all sorts of horizons . . . I realized that having a tongue ring did not make you scary—that's quite a lot for a girl from Iowa.

Graduate, English, Simon's Rock College of Bard

**I felt like I was by myself** as people on my floor started finding groups. I wasn't much of a drinker . . . and then, you always wonder if it's a race 'thing.' I was thinking of transferring. Then I joined a cycling club, something I love . . . and things just kinda fell into place. I'm glad I stayed.

Senior, History, Marquette University

> ## "I felt like I was the stupidest, poorest person on campus my freshman year."

Graduate, Biopsychology, University of Michigan

I was surrounded by kids who were phenomenal and I just wasn't getting it. **I was doing everything I was supposed to and still flunking.** It wasn't until my sophomore year that I really felt like I fit in . . . that I could do it. I had been just angry enough that I wasn't gonna let it beat me and that's what kept me going until I found classes that I loved.

Senior, Sociology, Harvard University

> "There's no reason to fail—NONE! There are people here to help and it's free. *Actually,* you've paid for it, every single thing, so you might as well use it."
>
> Senior, Education, Michigan State University

**I was 'the stuff'** in high school. In college, it was like 'Whoa, this is the 'Pros' . . . I'll look really stupid going to the tutoring center.' Eventually, it was obvious that what was really stupid was NOT going.

Graduate, Psychology, Spelman College

**It was like private tutoring.** There were office hours after class every day, but nobody ever used them except me.

Graduate, Ferris State University

ADVISOR

# HELP!

**Learning Center.** Determine your particular learning style and develop better test-taking, note-taking and reading skills.

**Writing Center/Help Rooms.** Help is provided for writing papers and web projects and tutoring sessions are offered for specific subjects.

**Mentoring.** Students are 'connected' to a faculty member or an upperclassman who offers insight and encouragement on an informal basis.

**Career Center.** Assessment tests and counselors will help you clarify goals and examine appropriate careers/majors.

**Counseling Center.** Help is provided for personal concerns, anxiety, substance abuse, eating disorders, sexual assault and other issues.

*Note: 37% of students who drop out have GPAs of 2.5 or above. For reasons other than academics, they have not "connected" in the college setting. (Levitz & Noel National Dropout Study)*

# Carpe Diem, Definitely!

*Seize the day!*

**The phone number on one little flyer** that I noticed my freshman year just grew into a 'dream position' I've had all four years. The people I've met and the doors it's opened have been incredible.

Senior, Film Production, Penn State University

**College was no bigger than my dorm** during my freshman year. I finally got involved in a campus group, and through that, a research project. There's a lot of cool stuff on campus . . . you just need to find it.

Senior, Physiology, Michigan State University

**All anyone wanted to talk about during job interviews was what I'd done outside of class.**

Graduate, Engineering, University of Michigan

# READ everything!

Bulletin boards, flyers, the campus newspaper, email—I didn't pay much attention to any of it and I missed a whole lot of things because I didn't . . . **I could have been scuba diving** in San Salvador for my natural science requirement!

Graduate, Humanities, Michigan State University

**I *totally* missed orientation**—didn't even know there was one! All kinds of good stuff can ONLY be found on the school website. You have to sift through it regularly.

Freshman, Lansing Community College

**HELLOOO** . . . you're paying $45,000 a year for more than going to class and eating in the cafeteria.

Senior, History, Marquette University

I went from playing sports and being active in lots of other high school activities to doing pretty much nothing in college. It took me awhile to realize that **you don't just sign up for stuff in 'homeroom'** . . . you have to get off your butt and find it.

Junior, Social Work, Rutgers University

*"I thought all the activities and clubs on campus were stupid because they didn't really do anything. Now that I'm in a career, I realize THAT was what THIS is all about."*

Graduate, Economics, Carleton College

**It was really cool to wave at the president** of the university and have him know who I was ... Being active in campus groups introduced me to 'key' people and opened a lot of doors.

Graduate, Communications, Weber State University

**A friend dragged me to a meeting . . .** I'd never even heard of the group. It ended up being my focus in college! I've gained so many skills and so much confidence ... more than in the classroom—and it's been more fun.

Junior, Business, University of Wisconsin

> **People are the best part. Having friends makes college easier.**
>
> Sophomore, Education, Vanderbilt University

**Sign up for dorm rep or join a committee . . .** you'll get to plan the social events AND the funds to do it! We did great stuff—trips into the city, "munchies" once a week. You meet a lot of people and find out everything happening on campus!

Senior, Business, Northwestern University

**The best part of college** has been Swing Club . . . as in dancing! It gets me away from the 'grind' and I've become good friends with kids in other majors—it's a nice opportunity to get a different perspective.

Senior, History, Weber State University

## Be a sport.

**Intramural sports are a blast . . .** you meet tons of people! Nobody takes it seriously. The only ones with actual 'plays' are grad students and ROTC'ers . . . kinda scary.

Junior, Economics, Northwestern University

**Don't overlook the obscure varsity or club sports . . .** the perks are the same whether it's football or fencing. I've made great friends, traveled, and I get to register early!

Junior, Michigan State University

**I've gotten to know upperclassmen** because of playing a sport. They not only tell you 'what's up' but will give you a ride there.

Sophomore, Premed, Cornell University

## Give it a shot!

**Who would have thought** I'd be auditioning for the Manhattan School of Music!?! I'd never even been in the high school choir let alone sung on stage until I got to college and decided to 'give it a shot.'

Senior, Education, Central Michigan University

**If I had it to do over** I'd have gone to more than just football games and parties. There were excellent speakers, concerts, theater *all right there!* Those things aren't available to me now . . . and for sure, *not at student prices!*

Graduate, Marketing, University of Wisconsin

*"It may be the only point in your life that you'll have the time and your parent's money to do it"*

# GO GLOBAL!!!

**I'd sell my car and everything I own** to repeat the experience I had in an overseas study program! I learned more during that semester than all the rest put together.

Senior, English, Denison University

Note: ccisabroad.org, iie.org, and studyabroad.com are among many online sites where scholarships are available for overseas study.

## Service Learning . . . the real world

**Volunteering in the community** has not only allowed me to test my skills, but it reminds me why I'm in school. I can go six stops on the subway from Harvard Yard and I'm able to link classroom theory with real people. The change of pace keeps me sane.

Senior, Sociology Harvard University

**I tutor math at a local grade school . . .** it's like a mini-vacation for me. It gets me off campus and I don't have to think about school.

Senior, Engineering, MIT

Note: Community volunteer opportunities are available through 'Service Learning' programs on most campuses.

## Cancun . . . of Appalachia? Alternative Spring Break

**Everyone else came back with a tan.** I came back with amazing stories of people that I had met at a shelter for political refugees. It was an awesome experience . . . an eye-opener. I learned so much about international politics and gained a real sense of my place in a very big world—all in a week!

Junior, Journalism, University of Michigan

## "At least one spring break ought to be something other than endless drinking and spending money..."

www.alternativebreaks.org

"Choosing courses can make or break you in college. The better you are at it, the better your grades and the less your aggravation."

Junior, Sociology, University of Colorado

# Choosing Courses

## In the beginning . . .

**It's better to take fewer credits** and do well than to just get by with more. GPA's are too hard to bring up!

Junior, Human Development, University of Connecticut

**The number of courses is more important** than the number of credits you take. Four courses worth 16 credits are more manageable than five courses worth 15 credits.

Junior, Kinesiology, University of Michigan

**Don't schedule too many** heavy reading courses in the same semester, and definitely not more than one lab!

Sophomore, Pre-Med, Cornell University

I was valedictorian in high school, so it was pretty discouraging when I had to work a whole lot harder—**for C's!** I should have started with an easier load and built up some confidence.

Sophomore, Premed, Cornell University

## AP Smarts

My friend had tons of Advanced Placement credits and ended up taking all upper level courses his first semester. He almost flunked out! **AP courses don't always prepare you for college work,** especially the pace. If he had mixed in a couple of beginning level courses or retaken an AP class or two at the college level, his GPA wouldn't have been obliterated.

Sophomore, Advertising, University of Florida

**I CLEP'ed out of some required courses** just by studying a textbook over the summer and taking the test. It allowed me to fit music classes into my schedule that I wouldn't have been able to take otherwise.

Graduate, Engineering, Iowa State University

Note: Anyone can earn college credits by taking CLEP (College Level Exam Program) tests prior to enrolling. Check to see whether your college accepts them.

## Quick Tips

**"Continue a language immediately.** If you wait until the second semester, everyone else will be coming off the first . . . very fluently."

**"Register for an extra class.** After the first week or so, drop the course you like the least."

**"Don't let the title or course description fool you.** Some of the worst classes *sound* fascinating."

**"Be choosy.** If a class or prof doesn't seem 'right,' change sections or drop it immediately while you can still get another class."

**"Take electives.** They'll help you decide on a major and make college more fun."

## It's now or never . . .

**Man, there are so many courses** I wish I'd taken in college! I always kind of thought I'd like broadcasting . . . so how is it I never even took a course in it? What a waste.

Graduate, Marketing, Ohio University

**I wish I'd taken more courses outside my major.** Everything I did—tutoring, summer jobs, whatever—was with children. All for my resumé, nothing for me.

Graduate, Education, Central Michigan University

**The sailing course was an unbelievable experience!** I'll probably never get a chance to take a class like that again in my lifetime!

Senior, Psychology, Michigan State University

# Don't waste money on blow off courses.
# Take what you're really interested in.

Junior, Engineering, Notre Dame

**I chose my classes based on what my friends were taking** or who the 'easy A' professor was. In retrospect, I wish I would have taken the classes I was interested in and focused on learning something that I cared about. The academic part of college would have been so much more exciting.

Graduate, Business, Notre Dame

# From the grads . . .

**Whatever your major, DON'T blow off writing courses.** I'm an accountant and my whole job is WRITING! There's reports to my boss, reports to clients, memo's to the file, and you *never* leave voice mail messages—it's e-mail!

University of Michigan

**I'm an art major** who really could've used some marketing and sales courses. Not *every* company has a 'sales force.' You're it . . . plus a lot of other thing you didn't major in.

UCLA

**I use my communication course every day.** It taught me how to confront people without alienating them and listen to customers and 'hear' what they're *really* saying.

Milwaukee School of Engineering

# . . . the courses you REALLY need

**I'd rather be criticized in a classroom** than a conference room. I avoid talking in front of a group at all costs. A public speaking course in college would have been a lot better place to get over the fear.

University of Michigan

**I always knew I wanted a career helping people.** What I didn't realize was that if you reach any level of responsibility you'll be knee deep in figures and formulas. You *need* basic finance and accounting courses.

Boston College

**Every day's a 'group project' in the real world** . . . nobody does their own job *'by themselves.'* A course in small group communication should be *mandatory.*

Weber State University

"

Pick the professor, *not* the time of day.

Junior, Economics, Duke University

"

# The Perfect Schedule

A good professor can make the most
boring course on campus fascinating . . .
and vice–versa

Senior, Economics, Carleton College

I used to pore over the schedule book for hours trying to arrange the perfect schedule. **No way would I consider a class before 10:00 or after 2:00,** and definitely no Friday afternoons. I never even looked to see who was teaching the course. After getting 'hosed' on instructors a few times it finally occurred to me that my method might be flawed . . .

Senior, Economics, University of Connecticut

# NO EXCUSES!

**It's totally stupid not to check out professors and courses online**
before you register. I've chosen every class that way and I haven't gone wrong yet.
You do want to make sure that it's not one or two people with an 'ax to grind' over
a crappy grade so read all the reviews . . . and whenever you can, confirm them with
'real' people.

Junior, Biochemistry, Michigan State University

*"My all-time favorite professor always gets trashed in the reviews."*

Senior, Education, University of Texas

*"When you find a great professor, take every course he teaches."*

Junior, Labor Studies, Saint Joseph's University

Nothing grinds you more than a friend having the same class with another instructor who's a lot more interesting . . . and less work. **You'll kick yourself for the whole term.**

Junior, Economics, Duke University

ADVISOR

F R O M   T H E   A D V I S E R

# Know What You're Getting . . .

**Talk to whomever has had that professor** and/or course. Use Facebook to find them. Students often know better than advisers which courses and profs are the best.

**Check professor and course ratings at online websites** as well as on your own college's website.

- RateMyProfessor.com provides reviews of specific professors.
- Koofers.com rates the professor as well as the course, providing grade distribution and the frequency of homework, tests, quizzes and papers

**Find the 'hidden gem'** by talking to your adviser or using your school's blogs and online communities. Some of the best courses have unsuspecting titles or bland descriptions.

**Beware of empty seats.** If the only section that's still open has lots of seats available and it's not an eight o'clock, chances are there's a reason.

## Timing is everything

**Schedule classes back to back.**
You're less likely to cut.

Junior, Business, University of Alabama

**Schedule two hours between classes**
and use it as 'built-in' study time.

Senior, Biology, Occidental College

**Register for an extra class.** After the first week or so, drop the course you like the least.

Sophomore, Psychology, UCLA

**Summer is a good time to take difficult courses.** Instructors are more relaxed, classes are smaller and the competition is less. It's perfect for taking labs.

Junior, Engineering, Notre Dame

**If there's an online option, I take it.** It frees up my schedule for other classes. Plus, it's a logistics thing—I *hate* going across campus for a class and I *hate* classes before 10 a.m!

Junior, Operations Management, Ohio State University


**Take large lecture classes on the 'off' semester.** Classes are smaller, you'll know the good professors, and the curve's usually not as high. My life would have been far less stressful if I had taken Chem 101 then.

Sophomore, Engineering, University of Pennsylvania


**The 3 hour classes, one night a week are great!** It's one night not wasted screwing around in the dorm and the prof always lets you go early.

Senior, Marketing, Ohio University

## The 'key' to closed courses

**If you can't get into a class,** talk directly to the instructor. Say something to set yourself apart from the other 20 people who are trying to add it—mention a colleague who 'suggested the class,' talk about your 'special interest' in his area . . . whatever it takes.

*Senior, Marketing, Ohio University*

**If a class will fill** before my enrollment date, I find someone with an earlier enrollment and have them "hold" it for me. It takes a coordinated effort, but it's worth it.

*Junior, Packaging, Michigan State University*

**It was closed** but I went to the class every day, waiting for someone to drop. No one ever did, but the prof eventually took pity on me and let me in anyway.

*Sophomore, Psychology, UCLA*

## You decide . . .

**I like eight o'clocks.** I roll out of bed, throw on a sweatshirt and go. Then I can study in the afternoon when it's quieter and have my evenings free.

Sophomore, John Carroll University

**Eight o'clocks are the worst!** Nobody goes to bed before 2 a.m. Ultimately, you end up sleep deprived and cutting class. Guaranteed.

Junior, University of Florida

*"Set the AM/PM mode correctly."*

"You are basically *screwed* if you miss a math class!

Sophomore, Economics, Williams College

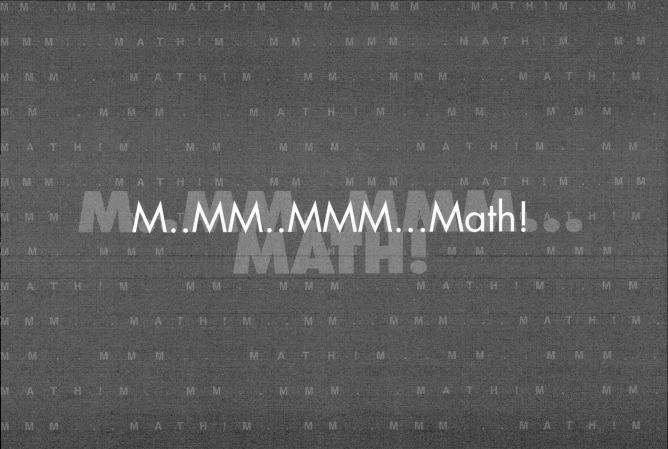

## Famous Last Words

**"Nobody collected the homework** so I figured I'd just wait and do it later . . . ."

**"I didn't want to waste money** taking the math I placed into, since I'd already had it in high school . . ."

**"I couldn't understand the instructor** so I decided to teach myself out of the book instead of wasting time in class . . ."

**"Math was easy for me in high school** and the first chapters covered stuff I knew, so I didn't actually work the problems . . ."

**"It was just a bad day** when I took the placement test so I enrolled in the next level . . ."

# CALCULUSkills

Even if you place into it, think twice before starting with calculus
*unless* you've had it in high school. Most of the class has, and
you'll be at a definite disadvantage if you haven't.

Junior, Economics, Duke University

Note: If that is the only math required by your major and a stellar grade isn't necessary, try it.

## Solutions . . .

**"Take math at a community college.** Classes are smaller."

**"Do practice problems** without looking at the answers first."

**"Look for small classes.** The seating capacity of each classroom is usually in the schedule book."

**"You can't cram for math tests.** It doesn't work. Keep up with the daily stuff so you won't have to."

**"Don't buy a calculator** without a backup battery."

**"Math opens the door** to some great majors. Hang in there."

## T.A. tips . . .

**Find a good one.** Most math classes have a common final so it's important to get a good T.A.—preferably one who helps write the final. Ask around. If the department won't tell you which section a T.A. you want is teaching, call him and ask.

Sophomore, Engineering, University of Michigan

**Change sections** if you really can't understand the T.A. But don't assume he's a bad teacher just because he has an accent.

Junior, Engineering, M.I.T.

**Some of my best profs** and TA's have been the ones with the 'worst' English. Don't let a litttle bit of an accent throw you.

Junior, Computer Engineering, Michigan State University

## Do-overs . . .

**DO NOT, for any reason,** go on to the next math level if you barely got through the first one. You'll get killed. Repeat the course.

Sophomore, Engineering, Central Michigan University

If you're lost after the first few weeks, drop back to a lower math. **I was beating my brains out** in calculus and barely getting a C. I dropped back to precalculus, got an A, and ended up getting an A+ the next semester in the same course that had been killing me before. I probably would have dropped out of engineering    if I hadn't been able to fill the gap between high school and college math. It's a big jump.

Sophomore, Engineering, University of Michigan

# The 'NEVER FAIL' Formula

***Before, not after.*** Doing assignments before lectures instead of after is the secret to math. I know exactly where I'm having trouble and what I need to learn.

Miami University

***Now, not then.*** Don't wait until you're totally lost to get help. See the instructor or get a tutor right away.

Western Michigan University

***All, not some.*** You have to be a maniac about math homework. Do *all* the problems.

Arizona State University

***Sooner, not later.*** No matter how well I understood things in class, if I waited a couple days to do the homework, I was lost. Do homework ASAP.

Albion College

" I was an expert at avoiding courses that required writing and at finding papers I could 'borrow.' When I discovered how much writing was expected at my first real job, I realized that it would definitely have been smarter to have perfected that skill in college. "

Graduate, Marketing, University of Wisconsin

# The 'Write' Stuff

## Foolproof fundamentals . . .

**Make it easier on yourself.** Choose a topic that you want to learn more about . . . or research issues related to careers you're interested in.

Graduate, History, Howard University

**Submit a rough draft.** ALWAYS ask the T.A. or the professor to review your rough draft before turning in the final paper. They're more likely to grade a paper favorably if they've 'helped' write it.

Sophomore, Art, Bowling Green University

**Make an outline.** Seriously. It's not a waste of time. . . it saves time.

Senior, Professional Writing, Michigan State University

**Confirm your thesis.** I put *hours* into a huge paper only to find out that I'd done it wrong! DON'T write a word until the professor has approved your thesis.

Junior, Business, University of Michigan

# "The only 'A' paper I've ever written . . .

. . . was when I thought the due date was a week earlier than it was. It was amazing how many times I 'tweaked' it during that extra week."

Sophomore, Criminal Justice, Missouri Western State College

**I try to revise every paper 3 times.** When you start early it becomes like your 'baby' . . . if you're late, you just want to get it done.

Junior, Economics, Northwestern University

# QUICK TIPS

Understand the assignment—'analyze' doesn't mean 'summarize.'

Don't proofread on your computer—review a hard copy.

Use the active voice rather than passive.

*Wikipedia* is not a citable source.

Know the URL of journals in your field so you can access the full text.

Flash drives get lost. Backup to an external hard drive or the Cloud.

When in doubt, Google.

## First impressions count . . .

**A good-looking paper is huge** with some professors . . . they're like 'OK, here's 10 points for extra effort.'

Senior, Business, Winthrup University

**You need to set the mood.** Make sure you're using the format your professor prefers—12 point type? Double-spaced? Margins? . . . *whatever!*

Sophomore, Undecided, Princeton University

*"Make your introduction awesome!"*

Senior, Sociology, Harvard

## Research the research

**Before choosing a topic,** check the Internet . . . you don't want one where there's very little information available or it's all pretty boring.

Senior, Economics, Notre Dame

**I *start* my research on Google** so I can get a basic understanding of the topic.

Junior, Political Science, Lehigh University

**Instead of spending hours sifting through websites,** I use the library's Help Desk. They know every conceivable resource and will help you find it.

Junior, Business, Western Michigan University

**I can access thousands of scholarly journals** and online resources using the library's databases and *know* it's good citable stuff. *And I can do it from my bed!*

Junior, Psychology, Georgetown University

*"A lot of people only go to the library to study or socialize, but it's amazing once you learn how to use it."*

Junior, Economy, Georgetown University

## according to the librarian . . .

"The library pays for the copyright on millions of journals and 'peer-reviewed' resources. You can trust the databases are reliable, factual and not just someone's opinion. That's not always true on the web. . . **there's a lot of funky stuff mixed in,** and you can't always access the full text without paying. We'll get you whatever you want, even if we have to order it."

*"It's just getting there the first time—once you go, you'll keep going."*

## The Writing Center

**I make at least two appointments** for every paper. It forces me to get it done on time and I'm really getting better at writing!

Sophomore, Political Science, Purdue University

**I just blocked!** I couldn't even get started! The tutor helped me organize my thoughts and gave me the confidence I needed to get going.

Freshman, Mott Community College

**I regret** not using the writing center like I should have. Whatever level you're at, they just keep making it better.

Junior, International Relations, Michigan State University

*"The Internet makes it easier to plagiarize . . .
and easier to get caught."*

# www.gotcha

As a member of the Student Conduct Committee, I've seen a lot of denials turn to excuses when we pull up the exact website that was copied. In the 'olden days,' instructors had only their suspicions when they came upon PhD-level work connected by 4th grade transitions. Now, it's like, **'Hey, Slick, we've got some pretty damning evidence here!'**

Senior, Government, Franklin and Marshall College

"I'd like to go back to my freshman year . . .
get some good grades . . .
make more intelligent decisions . . .
I just didn't have a clue."

Senior, Economics, University of Florida

# Get a Clue

# CLUE #1 Self-Discipline!

Dorm rooms can be a setup for failure. You're surrounded by every distraction you can possibly think of.

Junior, Geology, Arizona State University

## research shows . . .

**Self-discipline has more than twice as much impact on grades as does IQ,** test scores, school attendance, hours spent doing homework or the time of day students begin doing homework.

(Duckworth/Seligman, University of Pennsylvania, 2008)

**Our room is sweet!** We have a 40-somethin' inch TV, a PS4 and an Xbox One… kids are in and out constantly. The last thing I want to do is study…it takes a lot of self-control to pick up a book instead of a game controller.

Saginaw Valley State University

**There's always someone** who wants to do something. All I had to hear was, 'Wanna hoop?' and I was gone. After grades came I left my Nikes at home.

University of Toledo

**The good news and the bad news** is that you can just walk down the hallway and find someone to hang out with…'just gonna watch The Batchelor' turns into 2-3 hours of not studying.

University of Oklahoma

**Don't hang around people who do nothing but party** unless you plan a career in the family business or the local car wash.

University of Wisconsin

*"The first thing I do when I get up is check YouTube . . . then Twitter, then Snap Chat, then Instagram . . . and if I'm really feelin' it, I go to Tumblr."*

## www.what-a-waste

**You see guys spend hour after hour** in their rooms playing games online. It's like 'Wow! That's quite the social life you have there, pal.'

Junior, Political Science, Michigan State University

**All she does is sit and watch Netflix . . .** she doesn't even talk to us!

Senior, Kinesiology, Michigan State University

**I end up looking in Facebook albums** of people I don't even know!!! I can waste the whole night!

Junior, Psychology, Georgetown University

*"I'll have an assignment for 2 months and wait 2 days before it's due to start."*

## Pull the plug on *Procrastination!*

### A little self-help . . .

**Make a weekly 'to do' list . . .** *AND* every night make one for the next day. It's more productive to wake up with a plan.

**Make it specific.** Instead of writing 'Read book,' make it "Read pages 1-25.' Instead of 'Write paper,' make it 'Write outline.'

**Motivate yourself.** Think of a reason you need to get it done . . . a lifelong goal or just how good it will feel to get it done. Or, think about a latte you can't have or a party you can't go to unless you've finished.

My brother, who's not in college, works 40 or 50 hours a week at his job. When I'm sick of studying I try to ask myself if I've put in that many hours. It's **definitely a reality check.** You need to think of school as your job.

Junior, Engineering, Notre Dame

*"Where else is 15 hours a week considered a 'Full Load'?"*

T-shirt worn by Michigan State University Student

## RX: For good grades . . . *PAARRTY!!!*

College was the best time. . . **I never missed a party *AND* I got great grades!** The trick is to get up each morning and plan exactly what you want to do that night—party or whatever. Then tell yourself you can't go until you're done studying. It's like a reward. If I thought nothing was going on I'd waste the whole day and end up falling asleep in front of the TV at night.

Graduate, English, Ohio University

## Just sayin' . . .

**Seriously, college is way more fun** and you'll get way more sleep if you learn how to use your time.

*Junior, Politial Science, Lehigh University*

**If I'm just sitting in a classroom waiting for class to start,** I'll knock off a couple of homework problems. By the end of the day, I can be half done with the assignment.

*Junior, Kinesiology, Miami University*

**It sucks when I have a couple of hours** between classes and I end up playing around on my phone or computer instead of using that time to get something done. It makes that much more to do in the evening when I just want to chill with friends.

*Junior, Political Economy, Georgetown University*

# CLUE #2 Time Management!

I can't even say I'm on probation because of partying. I just became **a big couch potato.** For the first time in my life there wasn't anyone to tell me what to do or when to do it, so I didn't do anything—including study.

Freshman, Engineering, Michigan State University

# TIME . . .

**Study between classes.** I spent a lot of time watching TV during the day until I figured out that if I *studied,* I could have my nights free. Don't go back to the dorm between classes. Find someplace to study.

John Carroll University

**Stay out of bed.** Any time I didn't have classes, I slept. It's a *baaad* habit to get into.

Rollins College

**Prioritize.** I got so involved with club activities in my major that my grades were barely high enough to get *into* the major.

Michigan State University

# . . .Use it or lose it!

**Make a calendar for the entire semester.** I combine the dates from all the course syllabi onto one calendar and hang it where I can see it *daily*. It's a visual thing. You have to see it.

University of Wisconsin

**Set specific 'study hours.'** For me, the toughest part of studying is getting started. I set aside a specific time for every day. It's like going to a job; you *have* to be there.

Cornell University

**Make lists.** In high school you can do it when it comes to mind or when someone reminds you. In college there's too much to remember and *nobody's* going to remind you!

Adelphi University

*"I like paper planners . . . anything electronic gets lost,*
*stolen or falls in the toilet."*

## A daily planner keeps you honest . . .

**. . . I haven't exactly been the poster child for planning,** especially as a freshman and sophomore, but it's become my 'main thing.' College assignments are mostly reading so there's no homework to hand in. The 'I don't have any homework tonight' feeling can snowball instantly into hundreds of unread pages or a project you're just starting the night before it's due. My planner keeps me in touch with reality."

Senior, Government, Franklin and Marshall College

## Stress-busters!

**Break assignments down!** If you have a 400-page book to read . . . assign yourself so many pages per week. The end of the semester is *always* crunch time . . . don't make it worse!

Junior, Economics, SUNY/Stony Brook

**Gather all the syllabi** during the first week of classes and write down the due date for every single paper, project, test or whatever. You'll see instantly which weeks are potential killers.

Junior, English, Wake Forest

# " If you do nothing else in college, at least *go to class!*

Junior, Business, Miami University

*"I don't miss any classes with clickers. . . it's all about points!"*

**Even if I'd partied all night,** I dragged my body to class. Other people's notes don't work for me . . . I have to hear it myself.

Graduate, English, Indiana University

**Sitting in a classroom** is the easiest part of college and it cuts study time in half. Why make it hard on yourself—*GO!*

Senior, Journalism, University of Iowa

**Some instructors take it personally** if you cut a lot. Not having an attendance *requirement* doesn't mean they won't take it out on your grade.

Junior, Education, Central Michigan University

**They don't tell you ahead of time,** but at the end of the semester a lot of professors give extra credit for attendance.

Senior, Kinesiology, Michigan State University

I used to think the first couple of classes were a waste because everyone's still dropping and adding. **Wrong!** That's when the instructor announces changes in the syllabus and when you should decide whether to drop the class or change sections.

Junior, Business, University of Alabama

**Talk about horror stories . . .** I had one of those classes where you decide you'll learn more by reading the book than by going to class. I cut quite a few, including the one when a change in the final exam date was announced.

Senior, Communications, University of Toledo

> "It's not how smart you are—everyone is. It's whether you know how to study. I see really bright guys that get "nothing" grades and average guys that get 4-points.

Senior, Economics, University of Florida

# Grinding It Out

*"Of course it's hard! It's supposed to be hard!
If it wasn't hard everyone would do it!"*

—Tom Hanks, *A League of Their Own*

**It seemed like there was sooo much more free time** in college than in high school—until I realized that it isn't 'free.' You're supposed to be studying! It's just that there's no one there to tell you to . . .

Sophomore, Washington University

The first few weeks are great! You're meeting people, partying . . . no tests, no papers. Then . . . **WHAM!** *Everything's due in the same week!* If you weren't hitting the books right along, you'll spend the rest of the term digging yourself out!

Senior, Political Science, University of California, Santa Cruz

## Don't Get **BEHIND!!!**

The biggest difference between high school and college is the amount of reading. It's **impossible to catch up** if you get behind.

Sophomore, Biology, Kalamazoo College

# STUDYSMARTER...

**I'm studying 25% less** these last two years than I did my first two and my GPA is a full point higher. It took learning how and what to study.

Senior, Government, Franklin and Marshall College

**If you look at the chapter-end review** and all the chapter headings, they pretty much tell you exactly what you're supposed to be learning.

Saint Joseph's University

**Highlighters are overrated.** I can end up with the whole book in yellow and still not understand a thing. Taking notes and putting everything in my own words works better for me . . . and it's easier to stay awake.

St. Mary's College

**Avoid mindless reading** by outlining. It forces you to zero in on concepts and organize your thoughts . . . then that's what you study before a test.

New Jersey Institute of Technology

# . . . not harder

**Read your class notes FIRST** when studying for a test . . . THEN go over the readings. Your eyes will skim right past the crap and focus on what's important. If it wasn't mentioned in class, it probably won't be on the test.

Franklin and Marshall

**Keep asking yourself the same** question whether you're in a lecture or reading an assignment —'Will this be on the exam?'

Murray State University

**Go to discussion groups** even if they're not mandatory. It's easier to learn the material and it forces you to formulate your own ideas, which is very helpful for essay exams.

Michigan State University

**My roommate never studied** and got great grades. It took me a while to face the fact that I couldn't do that. It was frustrating, but that's life. You have to do what works best for you.

University of Toledo

*"There's always someone who likes to impress everyone with how much he knows. Include him in your group."*

## Study Groups . . .

**My study group saved me!** I could take the time to talk through something and people in the group would pick up on what I was missing. With 30–40 kids in a classroom, professors can't do that.

Graduate, Engineering, Milwaukee School of Engineering

**I don't believe in study groups.** The logistics are difficult and they waste time. The buddy system works much better. A friend and I have almost every class together. Before tests or writing papers, we bounce things off one another . . . between the two of us, there isn't much we miss.

Senior, Marketing, Ohio University

## Perfect timing . . .

Figure out when you're most efficient. **I was brain dead by 10 or 11 o'clock at night**—but that's when I started studying because that's when everyone studies. I'd have to read some things 10 times for it to sink in! Finally, I realized that studying during the day was a lot better for me—and faster. There are so many cool, fun things to do in college . . . you don't want to be studying all the time.

Senior, Engineering, MIT

*"I write better at night, read better in the morning, and my classes go better in the afternoon."*

Senior, Sociology, Harvard University

## Where to do it . . . (study!)

**Get out of your room!** You'll end up watching TV or cleaning out drawers—anything to avoid studying!

Rollins College

**Never study in front of an open laptop**—*and turn off your phone!* Stalking friends on Facebook and text messaging are both addictive.

SUNY-Stony Brook

**Studying in bed is an illusion.** After 15 minutes you're zonked.

Macalester College

**The library can be a great place**—or not so much. The stacks are totally quiet but the 2nd floor is like a singles bar.

Georgetown University

**The department libraries are great.** No one uses them except the brains.

Notre Dame

**I study for tests at Krogers**—I know too many people at the library. It's quiet, and when I need a break, I cruise the aisles and pick up samples.

Ohio University

*"I disable all my social media when I have serious studying to do.
It's like 'digital Doritos'—I can't stop myself!"*

**The case against DINGS, PINGS AND CHIRPS . . .**

- For every hour of electronic media exposure reported by first year students, GPA was reduced between .05 and .07 points. (Jacobsen and Forste, 2011)

- Only 65% of a 15 minute homework period was on-task behavior when social media was available to students. (Rosen, California State University, 2013)

- Students interrupted via instant message while doing academic work, were 20% less accurate than the uninterrupted group. (Acquisti and Peer, Carnegie Mellon University)

- It takes between 15 and 23 minutes to re-engage your mind whenever you are distracted by another activity. (Mark, University of California)

- Using social media while studying increases the amount of time needed to learn material and decreases the quality of the learning. (Junco, 2012)

"I'd sit in class and stare out the window at the squirrels.
They've got a cool nest in the tree.

Senior, Engineering, MIT

# Classroom Cues

## Little tips for big classes

**Sit front and center.** I can tell you what every person in class is wearing and not much of anything else when I sit in the back. Up front, it's like private tutoring . . . you get all your questions answered.

*Sophomore, Art, Bowling Green University*

**It was incredible how much easier Chemistry was** when I began reading the assignments *BEFORE* the lecture. It was like a different course.

*Sophomore, Engineering, University of Michigan*

**Always get the phone number** of at least one person in every class in case you can't read your notes or remember the assignment.

*Senior, Education, University of Tennessee*

## Big tips for little classes

**Don't be late or leave early.** It really ticks profs off. Besides that's when they usually make announcements or get to the point. The entire hour may be summed up in the last 5 minutes.

Sophomore, English, DePaul University

**I never miss sections or discussion groups,** especially close to exam time. TA's not only know what's on the exam, but sometimes have more influence over your grade than the professor.

Junior, Psychology, Georgetown University

**Volunteer to answer questions you do know** so you won't be called on for the ones you don't.

Junior, Psychology, Colgate University

*"I know when you're texting in class. Seriously, no one just looks down at their crotch and smiles."*

-The Prof

# PROFPOINTERS Classroom No-No's

**Don't ask questions** that show you haven't read the assignment. *DePaul University*

**Make eye contact** during lectures—at least, keep 'em open. *Indiana University*

**Don't ask,** 'What can I do to bring up my grade?' if you haven't been to class. *Rutgers*

**I hate excuses.** Tell it like it is and I'm likely to give you a break. *Albion College*

**Don't put down** other student's thoughts or opinions. *Michigan State University*

There were only sixty-three kids in my entire high school class—**no way was I gonna raise my hand** in a lecture with 300! Eventually I started keeping a list of my questions to ask the professor during his office hours...or I emailed him.

Sophomore, Advertising, University of Florida

**I have a hard time with 'class participation'** but I try to make up for it by talking with the instructor before or after class.

Sophomore, Psychology, Howard University

# WIRED! Online Courses

I hardly ever say a word in my regular classes; in online courses 80% of the grade is based on 'participation'. . . you *HAVE* to have an opinion and you *HAVE* to post detailed responses based on the assigned readings, which means you *HAVE* to read the assignments when they're assigned—

## there's no faking it.

Sophomore, Child Development, Lansing Community College

**Classes online made better use of my time.** I'm pretty self-directed, but if I wanted to make sure I was on track or needed a little help, I just popped into the actual class if it was offered.

Graduate, Professsional Writing, Michigan State University

**You have to READ, READ, READ . . .** and comprehend! There's no lecture to explain concepts . . .you're on your own.

Graduate, Psychology, Northern Michigan University

My online courses have all been 'self-paced'. . . **that's the good news and the bad news.** I love being able to learn on my own time, but it's easy to slack off and end up having to pull a bunch of all-nighters before the exam. It helps to 'schedule' study time just like it's a real class.

Senior, Communications, Michigan State University

# PROFPOINTERS E-mail Etiquette

**Don't avoid face-to-face conversation** by using email.     University of Oklahoma

**Delete all the unnecessary garbage** upfront and don't forward chain mail.

Oberlin

**It's NOT Twitter!** Use correct punctuation, spelling and grammer. A proper salutation and closing wouldn't hurt either.     UCLA

**I hate aliases.** Include your name, course and section.     University of Oklahoma

**I'm not going to do a lecture by email . . .** ask a classmate what you missed if you weren't in class.     Odessa College

**DON'T USE ALL CAPS!**     SUNY/Stony Brook

**Use your college email for school stuff** and a personal email account for everything else. Then you won't have to sift through a bunch of spam to find emails from your prof or adviser.

Junior, Psychology, Georgetown University

**There's no grammar check** on my email program, so if I'm responding to an assignment or a discussion forum that the professor will see, I write it in MSWord first, then 'copy and paste.'

Sophomore, Accounting, Northwood University

## Clickers: the good, the bad, the ugly . . .

I love clickers! It's easier to pay attention and I don't have to talk or sound like an idiot in front of the whole class but I still get participation points—IF I answer correctly. That's the catch...you have to read the material before class! If you cut class, you *can* send your clicker with a friend, but kids have been suspended for doing it.

Sophomore, MicroBiology, Eastern Michigan University

*"I have nightmares about losing everything on my computer . . ."*

Most schools give each student a large amount of online storage space—but they *never* use it! I did all the time!!! I saved all of my papers and projects, photos, power-point presentations... whatever. It's an excellent way to **back up all of your files** and be able to access them anywhere in the world—or just in the library.

Graduate, Professional Writing, Michigan State University

My laptop crashed the week of exams and there was no backup. Talk about learning the hard way . . . **Google Drive is my new best friend!**

Senior, Professional Writing, Michigan State University

# THE WEB VIRGIN'S GUIDE
## TO CAMPUS COMPUTING

- Password protect . . . so no one can use your computer without asking.

- Bring your installation discs from home in case you need to reinstall them.

- BACKUP! . . . to a flash drive AND an external hard drive or to the Cloud.

- Don't store your flash drive with your laptop—they'll both get stolen.

- Use a cable lock to secure your laptop.

- Activate your 'auto save' feature.

- Don't open unknown attachments—especially '.exe' files.

" Don't bring a laptop!
Even if you plan on taking notes,
you'll just end up surfing the web. "

Junior, Political Science, Michigan State University

# Notes On Note-Taking

**I always check to see if lecture notes are posted online** so I can print them out before class and use them to take notes on. It makes the lecture easier to follow and there's no guessing as to what the major points are.

Junior, Information Technology, University of Virginia

**I like to sit in front** so I can see the instructor's notes better and I can use my phone to take pictures of the PowerPoints or graphs or whatever . . .

Junior, Economics, Kent State University

**Not everything a prof says is important.** But if you haven't read the assignments before the lecture you end up writing down every word anyway because you don't know what is and what isn't.

Junior, Biology, University of Michigan

# Listen . . . Think . . . SUMMARIZE!!!

I had tons of notes—I copied every word the professor said. Actually, I was so busy writing that **I didn't understand a thing . . .**

Junior, Criminal Justice, Saint Joseph's University

**Watch the eyes.** If the instructor looks down at his notes before speaking, the next sentence is probably important.

Senior, English, Rutgers University

**Pay attention to when you're not paying attention.** It's impossible to keep your mind from wandering. Know when you're doing it and mark the spot in your notes so you can get the information later.

Junior, Business, Marquette University

**Rewriting messy notes** is a great way to study, actually.

Junior, Marketing, Northern Illinois University

# Listen for . . .

# KEY PHRASES

"to sum it up . . ."

"remember that . . ."

"in other words . . ."

"in my opinion . . ."

"the turning point . . ."

"notice that . . ."

"point #1, #2, etc."

"the basic reason . . ."

"a prime example . . ."

"in conclusion . . ."

**I lost a notebook** with six weeks of notes in it! Your name, phone, course, and section number should be on every book you own.

Junior, Political Science, Ohio State University

**Instead of doing nothing** between classes, I clean up my notes. If I don't re-read and clarify them sometime the same day, they never make sense later.

Junior, Labor Studies, Saint Joseph's University

*"I use a yellow highlighter for what's important and hot pink for what's really important."*

# Nail your notes . . .

**Speak up.** Don't be afraid to ask an instructor to slow down if he's going too fast.

**Date your notes.** It's easier to refer to your notes or compare them with others if they're dated.

**Be creative.** I use a four-color pen, draw pictures, whatever it takes to make notes memorable.

**One's good. Two's better.** If I miss a class, I get notes from two different people. It's easier to pinpoint which information is really important.

"In high school there were zillions of tests, quizzes, reports, extra credit . . . you name it. In college, it might be just a midterm and a final. If you mess up on one, your grade's shot!"

Senior, Education, University of Tennessee

# Test Tips

# Talk with the instructor before tests.

**The odds are against you on first tests** because you have no idea what to expect. I make a point of seeing the prof a few days before, just to make sure I'm 'focusing on the right material.' In other words, I want HOT TIPS. Taking a couple of "confused" classmates along makes him even more cooperative. Don't waste your time with TA's unless they know what's on the test. Some do, some don't.

Senior, Marketing, Ohio University

# 2 Find old exams.

**Hustling old tests is worth the effort.** Profs seldom change them much. Even if they do, an old test will tell you which concepts you're expected to know and how well to know them. Check with students who have taken the course, the department, fraternity test files, the library, or the professor himself.

Senior, Management Information Systems, Ohio University

# 3 You gotta UNDERSTAND.

**High school is memorization and regurgitation.** Here you have to think. I remember bombing the first test after studying my brains out. Some of that stuff I swore I'd never seen before. It's called 'applying the principle.' You have to *understand the concept* well enough to see how it relates to something you've never discussed in class. That's where most kids get killed.

Junior, Engineering, Notre Dame

# 4 Know the vocabulary of the course.

**T.A.s are looking for key words and phrases,** and not much else when there's 200 to 300 essay tests to correct. The more you use, the better your grade. Actually, if you don't understand the terminology well, you'll have trouble with multiple choice and true/false tests too.

Graduate, Marketing, University of Wisconsin

# 5 Make the most of quizzes.

**Quizzes are an easy way to boost your grade** because they cover fewer chapters. It's your chance to make up for what you're going to screw up on the final.

Senior, Marketing, Ohio University

# 6 Scantrons error.

**Computerized test-scoring isn't perfect.** Smudges can kill you. If your grade seems incorrect, ask to see the answer sheet. It meant a full grade for me . . .

Graduate, Physiology, Michigan State University

# 7 Learn from your mistakes.

**Some profs only post the test scores** and never return the actual test. It's a pain, but **ask to review the corrected test** in his office so you know exactly what you missed. Otherwise, you'll repeat the same mistakes the next time.

Sophomore, No Preference, Michigan State University

" Grades stress you out . . .
learning draws you in.

Junior, English, University of Maryland "

# The ABC's of GPA's

## Grade grubbing . . .

**Grade errors happen,** but most kids just figure they didn't do well on the exam and don't bother to check, especially if it's during the summer. The 2.0 I got in a class was supposed to have been a 2.5—not a big difference, but enough to get me off probation.

Junior, Communications, Michigan State University

**Always go over a test after it's graded** to make sure there aren't any errors and to see if you can "milk" it for a few more points. Just don't overdo it. Profs get ticked.

Senior, Psychology, Adelphi University

**Ask the T.A. to reread a paper** if you think it deserves a better grade. I've never not been given the extra points.

Senior, Hospitality Management, Michigan State University

**Ask for extra credit** or to rewrite a test or paper you've bombed. Some profs won't let you, but most will.

Senior, Accounting, Indiana University

## Don't question an instructor's grading in front of other students. He'll be reluctant to help you.

Senior, English, Denison University

## When "easy" doesn't do it . . .

**Tough courses psyche me up.** I'm more disciplined because I know I have to be, so my grades are better.

Senior, Accounting, Valparaiso University

**The trouble with "gut" courses** is that instead of using them as an opportunity to grab a good grade and boost your GPA, you just blow them off and end up getting a C . . . or worse. They really ARE easy if you GO to class and DO the work.

Sophomore, Economics, Williams College

## Things that 'Don't Count'

**Attendance.** Profs will hammer you on the details of anything you write or say if you haven't been coming to class even when there's no attendance requirement. An answer that is viewed as 'a good effort' if you're in class regularly is likely to be considered BS if you haven't.

Senior, Government, Franklin and Marshall College

**Homework.** Homework may only be 10% of your grade but it really impacts way more than that. It's not only your opportunity to learn, but if turned in regularly, it tells the instructor you're really trying. If you're anywhere close, you'll get the higher grade.

Graduate, Biology, MIT

# DROP it!!!

It's not a sin to drop a class. If you're in over your head, **don't take the hit** of a poor grade. It's discouraging and can ruin a GPA.

Sophomore, Premed, Cornell University

Note: Make sure you know the final date for dropping a class, with and without a refund, and whether it will affect your financial aid.

# Help, I've fallen . . .
## REPEAT RULES

**Repeat an "F" as soon as possible.** It's the quickest way to raise a GPA.

**Don't bother repeating a 1.0 or a 1.5** unless you know you can do considerably better than a 2.0—or a higher grade is required.

**DO repeat a low grade** if the course is a 'building block' for a series of courses you'll need . . . especially MATH, or if it's a part of your major.

**Repeat courses at a junior college.** The transfer repeat usually wipes out the original grade—at a cheaper price.

Note: Repeat rules vary among colleges. Check with your adviser.

An average student can get the same
results as a smart one if he
plays his cards right.

Senior, English, Denison University

# Gaining the Edge

**It's weird,** you're the one who's only eighteen years old, but it's up to you to make the effort to talk with Ph.D.s if you want them to get to know you. I always try to find out what they're into, what research they're doing. If it's monkeys . . . I ask about monkeys.

Junior, Michigan State University

**It's not 'sucking up' per se,** but it's definitely 'efficient' to get to know the instructor and what he does and doesn't like.

Junior, Psychology, Georgetown University

## *Don't underestimate the power of kissing butt!*

Junior, Sociology, University of Colorado

# THINK
# THINK
# THINK About it . . .

Your grade on everything you write . . . tests, term papers, whatever . . . gets down to one opinion—the instructor's. If he likes you and thinks you're putting in effort, it can be **the difference between an A and a C.**

Junior, Business, Miami University

## Attitude is everything . . .

**Instructors will bend over backwards** to help kids who are really trying. Make every effort to let them know you are.

Junior, Journalism, University of Iowa

**If you go in thinking 'this sucks,** the prof's a dork,' you'll hate the course. Just sit there and figure you're gonna make the most of it. I aced a really nasty course that way. I stopped by the prof's office once a week just to talk. She loved me. Too bad I didn't figure that out in high school.

Sophomore, Lansing Community College

When there's a guest speaker on a topic or field
you're interested in, introduce yourself, shake his hand, get his email
and send a thank-you. He may or may not reply, but either way,
**the door is open** for you to contact him at a later date.

Senior, English, Aquinas College

**PROFPOINTER . . .**

*"I'm always amazed at how difficult it is to find a student
willing to be the representative to our faculty committee. . . the
networking and resumé potential is incredible!"*

–Michigan State University

# MENTOR magic . . .

A friend of mine worked on a project with one of our professors. That relationship eventually allowed him to accompany the prof to Poland and to present research to several economic groups. He was later **recommended for Phi Beta Kappa** by the professor and ultimately accepted at a prestigious law school. I could have been the one volunteering for that project . . .

Senior, Economics, Hope College

## It's who you know . . .

**I wasn't exactly the best student,** by a long shot, but I had established a good relationship with an instructor in my major, and he recommended me for the internship. Voila! Six months in the Virgin Islands!

Senior, Hospitality Management, Michigan State University

## . . . and who you don't

**Grad school applications** ask for three personal recommendations from undergraduate faculty. I barely remembered any of their names! I know they didn't remember mine!!!

Graduate, Telecommunications, Michigan State University

"Find one person on campus who really cares
about you surviving . . ."

Senior, English, College of St. Benedict and St. Johns University

**What separated me from the masses** was 'connecting' with a faculty member. I didn't even know what the possibilities were until he laid out a 'roadmap' and showed me a few shortcuts to get there. He made learning about the field exciting and was always there to listen and offer constructive criticism. When my confidence was shaky, he reminded me that I could do it.

Graduate, Neuro-Biology, University of Michigan

## Make-A-Mentor

**Independent Study.** A one-on-one course with a professor of your choice. Just ask whomever you'd like to work with—or get a recommendation from.

**Student/Research Assistant.** Is there a professor who you enjoy or who teaches a course you're interested in? Ask to be a student assistant or to work on any research projects.

**Campus Jobs/Activities.** These allow administrators and faculty to get to know you. You'll have frequent, informal access to great advice.

**Seminar Courses.** Very small courses allow you to establish rapport with instructors so you can easily tap their wisdom and resources.

**Advisers.** There are good ones who will become great mentors IF you see them often and during non-busy periods. If yours isn't helpful, find another.

My biggest regret when I look back at college is not having used the office hours.

Graduate, Physiology, Michigan State University

**PROFPOINTERS. . .**

*"I'm more inclined to answer frantic emails the night before a test or paper is due if the student is more than just a 'user name.'"*

Georgia State University

*"Professors enjoy helping students who want to learn, but we're really annoyed by brown-nosers who waste our time."*

University of Pittsburg

**Learn who the professors are.** If one of them is an expert in a field you're interested in or he's from a grad school you're thinking about, then he's the one you want to get to know and his recommendation is the one you want to have.

Graduate, Biology, Columbia University

**You can cut study time in half** just by chatting with instructors during office hours. They'll pinpoint what is and what isn't important in the lectures and readings. Most are glad to talk with you since they have to be there anyway.

Senior, Education, University of Tennessee

**Before asking** a prof for help, read the assignments. It's obvious if you haven't, and she'll resent you wasting her time.

Senior, Political Science, Western Michigan University

# PROFPOINTERS

## Who impresses 'em . . .

**I'm impressed with students** who make a point to introduce themselves and tell me their goals. Chances are I can help them get there or I know someone who can.

University of Connecticut

**I like to see students who have an interest** outside of themselves and their grades. They have something that I can learn from them.

Michigan State University

**The students who really impress me** may not be the "best" students . . . they're the ones who are really interested. Their focus isn't on grades as much as on really learning.

Iowa State University

**Some students seem to stay connected** even after a class has ended—they e-mail, stop by . . . whatever. I enjoy following their progress, giving them advice, writing recommendations.

Miami University, Ohio

# . . . and who doesn't

**It's a dead giveaway** when students ask questions designed to find out how little they can get by with. "How many pages do I have to read?" tells me that you're not very interested in a subject that is my life's work. Michigan State University

**I'm not gonna go the extra mile** for students who give me even the slightest signal that they're not interested in my subject. If you're not, you'd better fake it.

Texas A & M

**Students who don't go to class** are a total turnoff. I write 'em off.

Bowling Green State University

**It's interesting** that my full-time college students always give excuses for late papers and missing classes while my part-time students who are working and raising families seldom do. University of Tampa

" It's tough to have to lay out a "plan"
when you don't know where you're going. "

Senior, Economics, University of Connecticut

# The Major Dilemma

## Make a 'major' move.

**I probably spent more time checking out used cars** than checking out majors. I worried about it a lot but I never got off my butt and did anything to find out what each major was really about. When the time came that I had to decide, I didn't have much more information than I did as a freshman—it was kind of like throwing a dart.

Senior, Economics, University of Connecticut

**I could kick myself** for taking the Career Decision-Making course as a senior instead of as a freshman or sophomore! I've learned so much about careers and majors—and even more about *me*. I didn't even know the course existed!

Senior, Psychology, Michigan State University

# Strategies for Making Choice

**Talk to professors in courses you enjoy** about what majors and careers are related to that field.

**Know what's available.** In addition to the majors, get a list of minors, cognates, specializations, or whatever. They add focus to a degree and make you more marketable.

**Go to Career Fairs** and Grad School presentations. You'll get an idea of what's out there and how to position yourself for it.

**Use the career center.** Counselors and assessment tests may help you find interests you never knew you had or careers and majors you never knew existed.

**Talk to people in the career** you think you'd like about what's going on in that field and how to get there. Ask to job shadow.

*"I love _____ but I don't know how I'd make a career of it."*

(Sports, music, cars, nature, computers — whatever your interests.)

# IMAGINE

## How could I be paid to:

- Write about it?
- Perform it?
- Create a product related to it?
- Provide a service to people interested in it?

- Talk about it?
- Assist people who do it?
- Sell a product related to it?
- Learn about it?

Note: Adapted from Patrick Combs' Major in Success (Ten Speed Press, 1994)

# "There I was, about to graduate with some random degree . . .

. . . and feeling like I'd wasted my parents' money, when someone mentioned that my band could use the sound studio on campus if we knew someone in the media production major. **Whoa...how did I miss *that* major???** Probably, because I never took the time to see exactly what majors were offered—and actually, I'd never considered doing anything but 'performing' music. I'm now working on my 2nd bachelors degree and loving it . . . *and paying for it!*

Post-graduate, Media Production, Northern Michigan University

## Do your thing . . .

**. . . not your parents'.** If your parents want you to be a biologist and you're an artist, you'll never stay awake studying. It's too hard to get decent grades if you don't like your major.

Junior, Sociology, University of Colorado

**The money motive.** Don't make choosing your major a "career move." Pick what you really enjoy. Chances are the money will follow. If it doesn't, at least you'll like your job.

Graduate, Economics, Carleton College

**The tunnel-vision trap.** I just picked a major and stuck to the requirements so I'd be sure to graduate in four years. I keep thinking there were other majors I'd have enjoyed more . . .

Senior, Political Science, University of California, Santa Cruz

## Get real . . .

**Until the day he flunked out,** my roommate insisted that he was an 'engineering major'—completely ignoring the fact that he was pretty bad in math and science. If he'd been realistic about his major, he'd still be here.

Senior, Accounting, Indiana University

**Due to a lot of screw-ups my freshman year,** my major isn't exactly what I'd like it to be. Unfortunately, by the time I decided what that was, I'd already taken—and bombed—some of the required courses. It's like if you're even thinking about a major, find out the requirements!

Senior, Economics, University of Florida

*"Extraordinary drive comes from doing what you enjoy."*

Patrick Combs

# EXPERIENCE Counts . . .

**Internships are where it's at.** Mine helped me figure out that I hated accounting, and it also helped me get my first job. It's a good way to test the waters and build a résumé.

Graduate, Business, Albion College

**I'd have given up** on an engineering degree because of all the math if I hadn't had a summer job with an engineering firm. It made me realize that's the career I really want. Now I'm willing to do what it takes to get there—and that's math.

Sophomore, Engineering, Michigan State University

> **Forget Burger King . . . find a summer job or volunteer doing something related to a career you may be interested in. It'll help you decide whether you are.**
>
> Junior, Business, Marquette University

**I'd be heading to grad school in the wrong field** if it weren't for one thing—volunteering! I had no experience in anything other than retail sales until this fall when I started volunteering at a local agency. Everyone says, 'find your passion.' I think I have . . . just in the nick of time.

Senior, Psychology, Michigan State University

I always wanted to be a nurse—I thought.
It wasn't until I started working in a hospital,
AFTER struggling through a year and a
half of tough science courses, that I realized
**I don't even like being around sick people!**
A little volunteer work or summer job would
have told me that a lot sooner.

Junior, Education, University of Michigan

## For love . . .

**My parents were so worried** when I told them I wanted to major in animal science. They were afraid that since I had decided against vet school I would end up doing kennel clean-up at $8 an hour. I loved animals and stuck with my plan . . . it worked! I'm a drug rep to veterinarians so get to help animals every day.

Graduate, Animal Science, Ohio State University

## . . . or $$$

**I followed the money.** Was I right? Well, no. But I wasn't really wrong either. I'm not in love with my job every single day, but it gives me freedom and yes, the money, to do what I love outside of the office. It's a happy medium.

Graduate, Finance and Business Economics, Notre Dame

**My advice is DON'T wait** until your senior year to find out what the job prospects are in your major. If it's highly competitive, there are things you need to do along the way to make yourself more marketable—pick up a minor, learn a language, volunteer . . . whatever.

Senior, Economics, University of Connecticut

**Find out which majors** at your school are considered 'tops' in their field. You might run across one you'd really like . . . and graduates from those majors are usually heavily recruited.

Graduate, Packaging, Michigan State University

*"You just need to take one step at a time. If it feels right, keep going.*
*If it doesn't, change directions. Ultimately, you'll be headed the right way."*

## THE BIG PICTURE

You can be totally immobilized if you think of choosing a major
as what you're going to do with **'the rest of your life!?!'**
For most people, it isn't. Looking back, I think it makes sense to
choose a major based on what you enjoy. You're more likely to be
enthusiastic and that's what opens doors. Besides, most entry-level
jobs require skills you'll learn in ANY major.

Graduate, Business, University of Tennessee

## Bottom Line: A JOB

Unless you're in engineering or accounting, or something specific like that, majors are pretty much interchangeable when it comes to getting a job. Eight of us were recently hired in this company, all with different majors.

Graduate, English, Indiana University

Note: 80% of students will be working in a field unrelated to their major within 10 years of graduation.

## Senior year . . .

**I don't even know what kind of job to look for,** let alone where to find it. I wish I'd majored in something that directed me to a specific career—teaching, dietetics, accounting, something like that.

## . . . one year later.

**I landed a great job** that has absolutely nothing to do with my major. I got it because of my work experience, campus activities, and good recommendations from both.

Graduate, Humanities, Michigan State University

" When you first start college,
you don't even know what questions to ask
because you don't know what
you should know . . ..

"

Senior, Education, St. Mary's College

# Surviving 'The System'

## Who has the answers . . .?

**Be kind to secretaries.** They can make your life a lot easier and usually know more about the rules and regulations than instructors.

Senior, Film, San Francisco City College

**I always started with the R.A.** If she couldn't answer a question, she knew who could.

Senior, Economics, Carleton College

**The campus website is an amazing resource** for info on just about anything—courses, events, buying books, finding tutors . . . whatever.

Sophomore, Aquinas College

**There are advisers and there are advisers.** The best thing I did was find one who was willing to do more than just okay my schedule.

Senior, Economics, University of Florida

# That's a Good Question . . . Ask it!

**What's the last day** to add or drop a class—with and without the 100% refund? Is a drop noted on the transcript?

**What are the minimum number of credits** allowed to maintain eligibility for financial aid, scholarships, academic honors, health insurance, or living in the dorm?

**What are the deadlines** for application to various majors?

**Is a 'repeat' averaged** with the original grade or does it replace it? How many repeats are allowed?

**Can courses be taken for credit only,** no grade, otherwise known as pass/fail? Will all majors accept them?

## Get It In Writing!!!

**Universities are notorious for screwing up.** Keep all your receipts, copies of drops, adds, anything that you had to get official permission to do.

Senior, English, Rutgers University

Someone I saw my freshman year told me—or I thought she did—that I could substitute one of my requirements with another course. By my senior year, whoever it was, was gone and **there was nothing noted in my file.** I had to take the course.

Senior, Marketing, Ohio University

**If you're sick,** don't just lie around your room until you're better. Notify the instructor and see a doctor at the health center to get medicine AND verification. Profs are leery of scams.

*Senior, Business, University of Toledo*

**Pre-register!!!** Grab what classes you can even if you're unsure. You can drop and add later.

*Junior, Geology, Arizona State University*

**'I' is better than 'F.'** If it looks like there's no way you'll be able to complete the work on time, ask the instructor for an 'Incomplete.' It's worth a shot...just be prepared to 'suck it up' over break and get it done. Don't drag it into the next semester!

*Senior, Environmental Studies, Michigan State University*

# Transfer tips, tricks . . .

**Don't hesitate to transfer** if you can't get into the program you want. I knew I wanted to be a teacher, so when I wasn't accepted, I transferred. In the long run, no one cares where your degree's from.

Eastern Michigan University

**Be prepared to hit the ground running** when you transfer as a junior. Grades don't transfer so you'll only have four semesters to establish your GPA. and it will be based on all upper level courses.

University of Colorado

**Keep in touch with advisers** at the school you want to transfer to. They'll tell you exactly which courses you should be taking and they'll know you're serious about transferring.

El Camino Junior College

**I felt like a 'freshman'** with junior status when I transferred . . . I was lost. Believe me, you're pretty much on your own— there's no big orientation. Get involved in activities and make a point of connecting with faculty as soon as possible.

Michigan State University

# . . . and traps.

**Credits transfer, grades don't**—which makes community colleges a good place to take tough courses without destroying a GPA. Classes are smaller too, so you're likely to get more attention.

University of Florida

**Beware of 'equivalents.'** No way did the course I took at another college during the summer prepare me for the follow-up course at my own school. It's better to take the last course in a sequence at another college, not the first.

University of Michigan

**When you're 'explaining'** a course you've taken somewhere else to the person deciding whether to accept that credit, make sure you know the *description of the "equivalent" course* at that school. A few well-chosen words or phrases can make all the difference.

Ohio University

**Do it *before* you're a junior** if you plan to take a course at a community college. Credits from a two-year school may not be accepted after that.

Michigan State University

Note: Transfer rules vary from college to college. Check yours.

It's amazing how many things on this campus would really have been helpful if I'd known about them as a freshman instead of a senior . . .

Senior, Accounting, University of Michigan

*There are all kinds of people on campus that get paid to do random stuff to help students . . . it's their job!*
*You just have to find them.*

Junior, Political Science, Michigan State University

F R O M   T H E   A D V I S E R

# Places to Go . . . People to See

**Learning Center.** Develop strategies for better test-taking, studying, note-taking, reading, etc.

**Service-Learning.** You'll find opportunities for volunteering in community agencies, schools, business, government, etc.

**Student Services.** Get information on research opportunities, mentor programs, student organizations, and overseas studies.

**Career Counseling.** Assessment tests and counselors will help you clarify goals and examine appropriate careers/majors.

**Job Placement.** Access employers on and off campus, summer jobs and internships.

Note: Not every college refers to these services by the same name.

# GOODadvice

If I'd talked to an adviser instead of just my friends **I could have saved about $5,000** and a lot of grief. Between the classes I took that I didn't need and the semester I added by missing the application date to my major, a few visits to the advising office would have really paid off.

Senior, Nursing, Michigan State University

**Don't believe everything you read.** The printed requirements for majors aren't always up to date, or they'll accept a course that's not listed. I took a class I hated only to find that the requirement had been dropped.

Graduate, Michigan State University

**You can mess up your graduation date** if you miss a course that isn't offered every semester, especially if it's a prerequisite for other courses you need! Have an adviser review your four-year plan.

Junior, Chemical Engineering, M.I.T.

## even better . . .

Don't wait until the last minute to see advisers or professors. That's what everyone does, so they're too busy to help you beyond the bare minimum. On a slow day they'll give you all kinds of help.

Graduate, Business, University of Tennessee

**My adviser didn't have much advice** but my roommate's adviser was *awesome!* So, I just started seeing her . . . you need to find another adviser if you're not getting your money's worth.

Sophomore, Political Science, Purdue University

**I see my adviser for signing stuff** and approving my schedule, but when I want to talk about courses and career strategies in my major, there are a couple of instructors who really know what's going on in the field and are great to talk with.

Senior, Hospitality, Georgia State University

**I email my adviser** when I have a quick question; if it's more involved or I want to 'pick his brain' I like to meet with him in person.

Sophomore, Aquinas College

# face 2 face

I like it when students come to my office; I can dig a little deeper
and get a sense of who they are . . . that doesn't happen with email.
When employers and former grads ask me to recommend students for openings in
their organizations, or faculty members call looking for help with projects,

**it's the students that I've talked with face to face that I recommend.**

-The Adviser

" Everyone we interview has a 3.0.
So what makes you different? "

Job Recruiter

# Smart Moves

## Head's Up . . . Networking!

**You can tell who's going to go places**—they not only have good technical skills but they network like crazy.

Senior, Electrical Engineering, MIT

**I'm glad I checked around . . .** I found that the doctor at one of two animal clinics I was considering for a summer job was not only on the admissions committee at the Vet School but was well known in the field. That's the clinic I chose! The doctor took me to trade shows and seminars where I got to meet anyone and everyone in the industry. I also discovered that I preferred the business end of veterinary medicine.

Graduate, Animal Science, Ohio State University

**Join a professional association** related to your major. That's how I know what's going on in my field . . . their newsletter and online discussion group. If I need good stuff for a paper or want to know who to contact for a job, it's easy.

Junior, Horticulture, Michigan State University

**I have the 'in' on everything** that goes on in theatre—*my passion*—because I work as the assistant to the college's producer. I'll always have amazing people to go to for advice because of it.

Senior, Architecture/Theatre, New Jersey Institute of Technology

**As a Student Assistant,** the professor treated me more like a colleague than a kid. I got all the 'inside info' and by teaching others, I learned the topic so well I could do it in my sleep.

Senior, Art, Alfred University

Note: Student Assistant positions are available through the department or by contacting a professor directly.

# JOIN! **Definitely join a club** affiliated with your major. That's
where you'll meet faculty and make contacts with people in your field. Guest speakers
are often just a year or two out of college so they're easy to talk to and usually willing
to forward resumés to higher ups.

Senior, Accounting, Indiana University

As an undergrad I joined a lot of **'low commitment-high resumé groups.'** The
reality is that when it comes to paring your resumé down to one page, that stuff
goes. If you've done zip in the group—there's nothing you're proud of—then
it's a waste of time.

Graduate, Communications, Weber State University

# DIY Do-It-Yourself!

**It started with four of us who wanted to learn how to make the next great computer game . . .** and now there are about 40 of us and weekly meetings! It's fun and a lot easier to have the resources and motivation of a group. I want to work in the computer game industry when I graduate but my concern has always been how to get IN! Companies probably get hundreds of e-mails and resumés a day asking for jobs. BUT, I gotta believe there won't be many applicants sending a CD full of demo programs they've helped create and a resumé that includes founding a game programming club at a major university.

Junior, Engineering, Michigan State University

**There's no downside to research projects.** You often get paid, the hours are flexible, it looks good on a resumé and letters of recommendation tend to be stellar! Start looking around for one your freshman year.

Graduate, Animal Science, Ohio State University

Because I was pledging a fraternity my freshman year, I decided not to take part in the research program I'd been invited to join—thinking I'd do it later. Well, I never got around to it. When I see how 'well-connected' and focused people are that are in it, I realize **I really screwed up.**

Senior, Biology, University of Michigan

100%
SATISFACTION
GUARANTEED

Nothing compares to the advice and encouragement you'll get and the connections you'll make when working with a faculty member on a research project.

Graduate, Psychology, University of Texas

# Think RESUMÉ

**I had 3 different internships** starting my freshman year. The variety really helped me define my career direction. AND because I'd had so much experience, I totally skipped the entry level position in my first job.

Graduate, Advertising, Western Michigan University

I always prefer job candidates who have had any kind of work experience, even if it's folding shirts at The Gap, to an applicant with only a formal education. If they've had an internship related to the field it's icing on the cake because **I know they understand what they're getting into.**

Vice-President of Human Resources

## Hey, there's no Santa either . . .

Everyone talks about *'getting an internship'* . . . I thought there must be some **'internship fairy'** that just appears and hands 'em out. NOT! There may be some available through your major or at the career center **but basically, you're on your own.**

Junior, Sociology, University of Colorado

# INTERNSHIPS . . .

**Cold Calls.** I just picked up the phone and asked for an appointment with Human Resources at a company I thought would be interesting to work at. I told them I'd work for free—which I would've—but they're paying me.

Michigan State University

**Upperclassmen.** Keep tabs on where upperclassmen and grads you know are working or interning. Ask them to pass on your resumé.

MIT

**Career Fairs.** Freshmen should definitely go just to check out what the possibilities are and who to contact. At least you know what you're gunning for.

Penn State University

**Internet.** A friend of mine found an internship with the Olympic Bobsled Team on the Internet. How cool is that?! (check out www.internshipprograms.com and monster.com)

University of West Florida

**64% of interns are eventually offered a job by their host employer.**

# . . . where to find them!

**Faculty.** I told my professor that I wanted to spend the summer in California and he gave me the names of colleagues I could contact for a job. Profs know people all over the country.

MIT

**Volunteer.** I set up my own internship with the Volunteer Coordinator at a local hospital. A friend of mine couldn't find a journalism internship so he offered to work on their newsletter.

Michigan Technological University

**Contact 'associations.'** Every career field has an association. Contact it for a list of intern positions—or ask if you could put your inquiry in their newsletter or listserv*.

Creighton University

**Friends and family.** It's always who you know . . . or who your parents know. But with friends of your family, you really don't want to screw up!

UCLA

*A listserv is an online discussion group related to a specific topic.

**My smartest move . . . taking a 5th year!** I could have graduated in four but by my senior year I was just getting on track. I was working on a great research paper with a faculty member and I'd just become a cheerleader. I'm convinced that the extra time I had to do those things is what made my application to an Ivy League professional school stand out . . . yep, I got in!

Graduate, Neuro-Biology, University of Michigan

**My smartest move . . . Honors College.** Coming out of high school it sounds intimidating or geeky, but it actually makes college easier. I got to register early so I had my pick of classes and professors, and I was able to create my own program according to my interests. As an Honors Student, people always bend over backwards for you.

Graduate, Professional Writing, Michigan State University

## ProfPointer . . .

Even as a freshmen you should be checking out career websites like Monster.com. . . . who are employers looking for? What skills do they want? What questions do they ask? **What do *you* want the answers to be?** When you determine that, you'll know exactly what you should be doing over the next four years.

Georgia State University

"I can still hear my dad's voice
after my first semester,
'What the hell are you doing with my money?'"

Junior, Economics, SUNY/Stony Brook

# Financial aid finesse . . .

I visited the financial aid office during the summer before my freshman year. Classes hadn't started so they weren't swamped yet. It was **the best thing I ever did.** The adviser took a lot of time with me and got to know my situation. From then on, I always requested him. Over the course of my college career, he saw to it that I got some serious cash.

**Graduate, Biology, University of Michigan**

**Get your FAFSA in early—like October of your senior year!** There's more grant money available and you'll find out that much earlier how much financial aid you can get from each of the colleges you're applying to. It made my decision pertty easy.

Freshman, Criminal Justice, University of Memphis

**Beg . . .** or at least, plead your case. Computers only know numbers and those don't tell the whole story. My mom had lost her job and couldn't contribute anything, let alone the $20,000 the government had calculated. Once the aid office heard the *whooole* story, I not only got the aid, but a scholarship!

Sophomore, Computer Engineering, Michigan Technological University

**Borrow only what you need** when it comes to student loans. I always took the 'max' since there were a lot of things I *needed*—a $1000 bike, a flat screen TV, a sound system—I'll be paying for them for the next 20 years!

Senior, Film, San Franciso City College

# "We have scholarships we can't give away . . .

. . . because kids won't write the essay. All they need to do is write a brief essay, list community involvement—and they get the money!"

Alumni Scholarship Fund Office

**I made $25,000 for ten hours of work!** My mom pretty much had to put a gun to my head to get me to fill out scholarship applications. I ended up getting two out of the 6 or 7 I applied for . . . nice hourly rate!

Senior, Engineering, MIT

**People don't think to apply** for scholarships to their churches or parents' places of employment (even if they don't work there anymore). And corporations are always generous. Here in Atlanta we have Delta, Coca-Cola . . . and Ted.★

Senior, Psychology, Spelman College

★ CNN's Ted Turner

# NEVER too late . . .

I'm so mad at myself for not applying for the scholarships that were available. I didn't get one as a high school senior so it didn't even occur to me to apply in college . . . **dumb!**

Senior, Human Communications, University of Connecticut

Note: There are private grants and scholarships available to existing students throughout college. They're usually through the department of your major, professional organizations or foundations. Check with advisers and sign up at www.Fastweb.com for email notices.

## Banking and Checking . . .

**'Account Alerts'** automatically email or text message you when your balance is low. Check to see if your bank offers that feature.

**Set up your checking account and debit card** with your parents' bank if it has a branch in your college town. Merchants and landlords don't like out-of-state checks, plus, your parents can quickly 'reload' your account.

**Get overdraft protection.** It's worth it—as long as you don't use it as credit. The interest can bury you.

**No matter what,** *DON'T* write your access code down on paper and send a friend to do your banking. *Borrow* money until you can do it yourself.

$90 in overdraft fees made me religious
about recording what I put on my debit card.
Forget what the online balance says . . .
it's like NOT always up to date.

Junior, Labor Studies, Penn State University

I feel like such a sucker every time I agree to pay $2.95 to access my own money. That's a **skinny vanilla latte at Starbucks!** Before opening a checking account, find out which bank and ATMs are on campus or convenient to you.

Graduate, Professional Writing, Michigan State University

## Credit Cards . . .

**Don't use a credit card** for anything you eat, wear, or listen to. Who wants to pay interest on a meal eaten a month ago?

**Do the math . . .** if you're only paying the minimum each month, the actual cost of the item is 3–4 times the original price.

**If you can't trust yourself** to pay *on time, every month,* don't use a credit card. There's a $30 fee and your credit rating's trashed.

**Never get a cash advance** on a credit card. The interest accumulates *daily* and will kill you.

**Use 'plastic' to pay tuition.** The Frequent Flier points are huge, which means free air fare to and from school—or *maybe* Cancun?

"We do a credit check on all job applicants before hiring. It's based on retail accounts, gasoline cards, rent payments—*but primarily on credit card history.*"

Vice-President of Human Resources

Credit cards are good to have in case of an emergency—*but* make sure you're clear on the definition of 'emergency.' For me it was every time I went into Express—**until my dad saw the bill.**

Sophomore, History, University of Pennsylvania

## Better Book Buying

**"I buy from the bookstore because** it's all in one place and I can see what I'm getting."

**"Buying online is usually *waaay* cheaper.** Just make sure to order the correct edition (ISBN) since YOU pay the shipping on returns."

**"I love ebooks...**they're cheap and I can highlight and make notes in the margins as much as I want! Studies show that real books are better for recall, but ebooks work for me."

**"Buy a previous edition of the book.** They're cheap and profs usually don't mind if there's not much difference between the two. It's worth asking."

**Renting books is the only way to go!** It doesn't really bother me that I can't write in them or use a highlighter…I take notes in my notebook and use post–its in the book.

Sophomore, Sports Marketing, Xavier University

**Renting online is too nerve-wracking for me.** The returns have to be postmarked by the exact date or you're charged full price…and the pages can't have any writing or 'excessive' highlighting. So what's excessive…?

Junior, Marketing, Northern Illinois University

**I buy my books after classes start** so I can see if any aren't really needed. You can't wait too long or you'll get behind in reading and there won't be any used books left to buy.

Senior, Bio-Engineering, Lehigh University

# A JOB !?!?!?

Don't get a job until after your freshman year . . . or whenever you've figured out how to manage your time.

Senior, Economics, University of Florida

## and the best job . . .

Get a job in the office of your major. You'll get to know everyone from the secretaries to the dean, all of whom can be very helpful. **If any great opportunities come along, you'll be the first to know.**

Senior, Environmental Science, Indiana University

**It's a trade-off.** I was working so many hours that I had to cut back on credits. In the long run, it's cost me. I'm taking longer to graduate and it'll be that much longer before I'm making real money.

Junior, Business, University of Alabama

**If there's nothing much to do,** I don't do much of anything, including study. I manage my time better when I'm working 15 to 20 hours a week.

Senior, Business, University of Toledo

**A job gets you 'out there'**—you meet more people and connect on different levels. Even if it's a few hours, it's important to work...or volunteer or do something.

Junior, Psychology, Colgate Universtiy

**The best thing** about being on financial aid is that you qualify for 'work-study' jobs. They're usually on campus so you don't need a car and your boss 'understands' when you need time to study. Actually, you usually can study on the job.

Junior, Marketing, Northern Illinois

# Q U I C K T I P S

"The good jobs go fast. Start looking early."

"Work your tail off in the summer so you don't have to work during the
school year."

"Find a job in something related to your major."

"Don't work in restaurants unless you wait tables. That's where the money is."

"Find a job where you can study."

"Don't work more than 20 hours a week if you're carrying a full load;
ten to fifteen is better."

# Cars on CAMPUS

**Parking on campus is a nightmare.** Out of desperation you always end up parking in restricted areas. I had to take out a short-term note just to pay off parking tickets and tow charges before I was allowed to register.

Senior, Telecommunications, Michigan State University

**I was so hung up on parking fees** that the minute class was over I was 'outta there'—I left campus. Study groups and just hanging out with other students didn't happen. College wasn't fun. I still don't like the parking fees but now I suck it up and stick around to take advantage of the people and resources on campus.

Sophomore, Lansing Community College

Note: Parents, you may be able to get lower auto insurance rates if your student is more than 100 miles from home and doesn't have a car at school.

Everyone's like,
'Oh that's not gonna happen to me' —
but it's in the paper every day.

# Crime Stoppers

## Keep your eyes on the prize . . .

**Label everything!** There's a guy walking around campus in MY $200 jacket, but I've got no proof. I'm ticked every time I see him.

Senior, Ohio University

**Don't leave your bookbag on a table** while you're in the food line! My computer, sunglasses, two graphing calculators and my class notes GONE—two days before exams!

Sophomore, Michigan State University

**Lock your door when you're sleeping.** My buddy was asleep with the door shut and someone walked in and took his game console.

Sophomore, Georgia State University

Note: Your parent's homeowner's insurance may extend to your personal property while living in the dorm.

*"Some people 'shop' in the laundry more often than the mall.
Don't leave clothes in the washer or dryer."*

**Use a computer lock even in your room!**  My suitemate didn't and her computer was gone. There's so many people in and out of the room, who knows who took it…

Junior, Western Michigan University

**I had my laptop engraved** with my driver's license number. Some colleges provide permanent registration stickers for electronics and bikes.

Junior, Rutgers University

**Ulocks are the only way to keep your bike safe,** and even then it might disappear piece by piece. Don't bring an expensive bike.

Sophomore, University of Oklahoma

## Avoiding creeps, perverts, & lowlifes

**Know the campus bus schedule** and plan on leaving before the last run of the night.

Michigan State University

**Stick to public places** when you go out with someone you don't know well.

University of Iowa

**Keep your finger on the button.** Mace or pepper spray won't do any good in your purse.

Columbia University

**Know how you're getting home** before you go!

Iowa State University

**Let people know where you're going** and when you'll be back. If your plans change, call.

Butler University

**Don't use ATMs at night,** especially if you're alone.

University of Pennsylvania

**Set up speed dial** on your phone for the university police.

Miami University

**There are four of us who use 'share your location'** on our iPhones. If I'm separated from a group of people or if I'm scared when walking somewhere alone, or even if I'm in a car alone and something's weird, I can ask one of my friends to watch and make sure I get where I'm going.

Sophomore, Michigan State University

**It's like TMI**—too much information! Harmless comments on social media like 'Everyone's partying, I'm home alone studying, yuck!' might seem like an invitation for some whacko you hardly know in your history class.

Sophomore, University of Oklahoma.

**Take a self-defense class.** It makes you more alert to your surroundings even if all you remember is to run like hell.

Junior, Lone Star College

"It's like there's this image of 'college' you need to live up to—wild parties, no sleep, cutting classes. It's easy to get sucked into, especially if you're not quite sure why you're here.

Junior, Geology, Arizona State University

# Partying & Stuff

# For the Record

**Really, you don't *have* to drink.** The only time people think you're weird is when you sit around doing nothing. Just go to the parties. No one notices what you do once you're there.

University of California/Santa Cruz

**Everyone's a little 'needy'** when they start college—you latch on to whomever. I spent every weekend drinking my brains out with the same people before I realized it was kinda boring.

Junior, Advertising, University of Florida

**We buy 3 pitchers of beer** and 3 pitchers of Coke. That's what college is about—making your own decisions. As long as you're around people who respect yours, it's okay.

Junior, Economics, Notre Dame

**Some schools can be anal** about the rules on alcohol in the dorms. Be sure you know the consequences. Around here you'll get busted big time.

University of Arizona

*You can always tell freshmen. They act like they've just been let off the leash.*

Senior, Business, Northern Illinois University

It's hard to believe what a straight-arrow I was in high school . . . National Honor Society and the whole thing. I've basically screwed myself so far in college. My entire freshman year 'went up in smoke,' if you know what I mean. I barely even remember the names of my courses, let alone going to them. **I guess the party's over—along with my scholarship.**

# The Unwritten Rule

**There's a responsibility . . .** friends take care of friends. You can do some dumb things when you're partying. Go in a group.

Senior, Biology, MIT

"DON'T BE SO STUPID THAT YOU ACCIDENTALLY DIE."

## Way Beyond Stupid

- Drinking a fifth of vodka through a beer bong

- Drinking and walking home alone

- Mixing prescription drugs with alcohol

- Drinking and driving

- Letting someone drunk drive you

- Drinking 21 shots on your 21st birthday

Excerpted from Harlan Cohen's Campus Life Exposed (Peterson's, 2000)

**A DUI will trash your career options.** You can forget being a pharmaceutical rep or having any other job with a company car. Even if you drive your own vehicle, your employer can be liable for any accident or injuries to and from meetings, which means they WON'T want to take the risk of hiring you.

Graduate, Central Michigan University

**The cops are really rude when it comes to MIP's.** My friend was drunk and just walking to his room—without any alcohol on him—and the cop gave him a MIP. That's serious... a $500 fine and his parents had to hire an attorney so that every time he applied for a job or grad school he wouldn't have to answer 'Yes' to 'Have you ever had a criminal conviction?' It also appears on your driver's record for 5 years.

Senior, Marketing, Michigan State University

\*MIP – Minor in possession of alcohol
\*\*DUI – Driving under the influence of alcohol

# Dating DILEMMAS

**If a girl even hints at 'no'** or 'stop,' pay attention. My friend was accused of rape, and even though the charges were eventually dropped, it was devastating to his family and he was dropped from the fraternity he was pledging.

Senior, Accounting, University of Michigan

Note: The highest incidence of sexual assault is among freshmen and is most likely to occur during the first 3 months on campus.

## "Don't take your ATM card to the casino."

## Know when to fold 'em . . .

**Sports gambling is huge** in the dorms and easy to get hooked on since it makes watching games with a bunch of guys really exciting. A friend of mine had to sell his Jeep to cover his losses . . . and that was calling 'lock lines' which are supposed to be sure things.

Junior, Criminal Justice, Saint Joseph's University

**All you need is a credit card and the internet** and you can get into some serious trouble. My roommate was major hooked on Texas Hold'Em until his parents saw his credit card bill.

Sophomore, Undeclared, Western Michigan University

College towns are exciting! You meet people from different backgrounds with different values. Know what yours are and stick to them.

Junior, Economics, Duke University

66

I wouldn't want to pay money
to have friends . . . but
fraternity guys do meet a lot of girls.

Senior, Economics, University of Florida

99

To be or not to be . . .GREEK

## Greek Musings . . .

**At some schools you're either Greek,** an athlete, or you sit around doing nothing on weekends.

Miami of Ohio

**It's a good way to make a big school feel small.** Classes at most universities are huge and you really don't get to know anyone. Sororities make it easier, less isolating.

University of Iowa

**Fraternities make it easy to socialize** when you don't have a lot of time. There's always a party or something going on.

Colgate University

**I've never worked so hard in my life.** We were forever fund-raising or doing some charity thing and someone was always griping about how it should have been done.

Michigan State University

**I'd miss a lot if I were wrapped up in a sorority.** I'd rather be involved in campus sports, clubs, plays and things like that.

M.I.T.

**It's a great network during and after college.** I have fraternity brothers all over the country. Someone's always got a father or an uncle who can open a door for you.

Colgate University

**I don't think it's worth it.** If you're worried about networking and resumes, get out in the community and meet people, get involved in a research project. That's likely to be more helpful in the long run.

Aquinas College

**Sometimes it gets to be too much.** You're always worried about your 'image.' Someone always wants to know, 'Who did you go out with?' 'What did you wear?' 'Who was there?' 'Why aren't you doing this or that?'

Indiana University

**Greeks always know what's happening on campus,** which courses are good, who's the best prof, job openings, parties. All that, plus test files!

Ohio State University

## What's the "Rush?"

**I pledged the first house I walked into** my first semester and spent a lot of time washing dishes and scrubbing floors before I figured out that it wasn't the place for me. Don't rush your first semester. Get to know guys from different fraternities and what's going on in them.

Senior, Accounting, Indiana University

**Forget which house is 'cool'** or who has the best 'national.' Look for people you're comfortable with. If you have to act like something you're not just to fit in, it's not worth it.

Sophomore, Premed, Cornell University

**My best friend didn't get a bid . . .** so I didn't accept mine. By the end of the term she had a boyfriend and I hardly saw her. I ended up wishing I was in a sorority. You need to do what's best for you.

Junior, English, Indiana University

*Pledging is like taking an additional four credits,
at least. Plan your schedule accordingly.*

Senior, Economics, University of Connecticut

Some fraternities make it impossible to get decent grades while you're pledging. **My G.P.A. never recovered.** If grades are your priority, make sure there's at least some value placed on academics in the house you're pledging.

Senior, Business, Northern Illinois University

# BEWARE of Greeks

Greek at one school can be totally different from Greek at another. Ours is big on parties, but sports, academics, and community service are big too. At my brother's school, **the houses are trashed and so are the guys** most of the time. Their idea of sports is playing Xbox while smoking a joint.

Senior, Marketing, Ohio University

**The biggest use of drugs** and alcohol is in the fraternities.

Junior, Geology, Arizona State University

**Everyone hazes.** It ranges from mild harassment to perverted and dangerous. Unfortunately you never know which until you're in the middle of it. By then, not only have you invested a huge amount of time, but you also don't want to look like a wimp by bailing out.

Sophomore, Advertising, University of Florida

After making it through a whole semester of pledging, our 'I' Week, otherwise known as **'HELL WEEK,'** turned out to be two weeks—one for the official initiation and another for the 'unofficial' one. The fact that no one was allowed to study during either, **forced two of us to decide whether we wanted to be Sigma Chi's or M.D.'s . . .**

Junior, Biology, University of Michigan

"College was what I wanted to do socially,
not academically.
I wish I'd taken it more seriously"

Graduate, English, Rutgers University

Ah Ha!

## Words from the wise . . .

Going to college was for my parents. It wasn't until I realized I was there for myself that I got serious. Unfortunately, that was pretty late in the game. **Somehow it has to become your goal . . .** the sooner, the better.

Graduate, Supply Chain Management, Michigan State University

**College was just the next thing** to do . . . and I could play soccer. At some point, it occurred to me that I really LIKED to learn and LIKED to talk to people about what they'd learned. I never knew that . . .

Senior, Sociology, University of Colorado

**I wish I hadn't put so much pressure on myself.** There were so many things going on that I missed. I should have relaxed, enjoyed it more, and done things because I wanted to, not because it looked good on a resumé.

Graduate, English, Indiana University

**College is the time to struggle** to learn a formula or a concept . . . it's supposed to be hard. That's how you learn to think, to problem-solve. Your boss probably won't be as lenient or as helpful as your professors.

Graduate, Finance and Business, Notre Dame


**Geez, where do I start . . .?** There are so many things I wish I'd done . . . I could kick myself for not realizing that college was probably the only time I'd have the freedom and the opportunity to explore options and try a lot of different things. After you graduate, it's all about paying bills . . . there's no time and no opportunity for much else.

Graduate, Marketing, University of Wisconsin

If I end up never being a biologist, I still wouldn't trade my life in college. I learned so much about who I am . . . what makes me succeed and what makes me fail. **It was an exploration of ME.**

Graduate, Biology, MIT

# WHAT IT'S ALL ABOUT . . .

**You don't 'get it' when you're in college.** It's not about what you major in or which classes you take . . . you won't remember most of them anyway. It's really about learning to think and to communicate. Wherever you end up, you'll need to be able to analyze and solve problems—to figure out what needs to be done and do it! 'Doing it' takes being organized, having the ability to express yourself effectively and a lot of other skills you didn't realize you were learning in some of those 'boring, senseless' courses. You can definitely scam your way through college without developing those skills . . . a lot of kids do . . . but in the long run, you're only limiting yourself. And believe me, that can make your first job a little scary.

Graduate, Marketing, Ohio University

**I have like thirty days until I graduate and I'm so depressed . . .** It took me until my senior year to appreciate the fact that I can walk right out my door and learn anything I want . . . ***it's all right here!*** College puts you in touch with so much . . . so many kinds of people, so many opportunities to try things. I'm more accepting, more open . . . . It takes every college student a while to figure things out, but I'd definitely say, 'Take advantage of the fact that you're there. Enjoy.'

Senior, Human Development, University of Connecticut

**"#\*@%!!!,** where was this book when I needed it?!?"

Senior, Business, University of Michigan

## SHARE YOUR TIPS

There's nothing better than the voice of experience. If you have any "hot tips" or words of wisdom you'd like to share, please do at

Front Porch Press
4733 Hawk Hollow Dr. E.
Bath, MI 48808
Email: styler@voyager.net
Phone: 888-484-1997

## Special pricing . . .

is available for our titles when purchased in bulk for educational, fundraising, or promotional use. Custom editions or book excerpts can also be created to specification. For details, contact Front Porch Press at 888-484-1997 or styler@voyager.net.

# Index

Front Porch Press also presents . . .

**Valerie Pierce with Cheryl Rilly**

# A TIMELINE FOR SUCCESS

This easy-to-follow timeline will help students maximize their high school years and optimize their chances of 'getting where they want to go.' While encouraging self-exploration and self-discovery, these 'to do's' provide the 'nitty gritty' details necessary to the college admissions process. There will be no missed deadlines or missed opportunities, as this step by step guide shows students and parents...

## WHAT to do . . . WHEN to do it!

For educational or group sales, contact:
FRONT PORCH PRESS
888-484-1997
**www.frontporchpress.com**

"It's what every tuition-paying parent wants their college son or daughter to know in a book they'll actually read!"

"I was a career counselor at the University of Texas for 7 years. Most of the students I served were seniors who were just discovering—*as they were LEAVING the university*—some of the things they 'should've' done to make the most of college. That was tough for me to see day after day after day . . . I love your book!"

"My friends passed it around for about 2 hours during the Super Bowl...they loved it! I couldn't believe it. Those guys don't read anything!"

"I'm a junior at Brown University and I picked the book up on a whim for my brother who's a senior in high school. I read through it and was amazed at how true the title is. It really is just about everything that I should've known before I left for college. If my brother really absorbs even half of it, he's going to have it ten times easier than I did!"

"It's some of the best college advice we've read . . . many thanks for providing such an honest and worthwhile book."

One of the many things I like about this book is that you can open it to virtually any page and pick up a great tip. It really reminded me of one of the many impromptu sessions I spent with my college buddies, trading experiences and talking late into the night—comfortable, easy-going, funny, and with a lot of great insights.  I definitely recommend it!

". . . a wonderful book . . . so realistic it almost scares me."

This book gives its readers some great nuggets of truth about truly living your college experience to the fullest. It is practical rather than theoretical and very easy to read.